PENGUIN VEER

IN HER DEFENCE

Navdeep Singh is a practising lawyer at the Punjab and Haryana High Court, Chandigarh. He is also the founder president of the Armed Forces Tribunal Bar Association in Chandigarh. Navdeep has been a volunteer–reservist with the Territorial Army in the rank of major in the past. He has been decorated with a record eleven commendations from the army, air force and tri-service institutions for his work for the military community and veterans and other issues confronting the defence services.

Besides constitutional and civil and military service matters, he has enthusiastically worked in the fields of rights of disabled soldiers, military widows, civil and military pensioners and on the subject of gender discrimination. He has worked for global reforms in military justice and improvement of tribunals in India. He has also dealt with landmark litigation on tribunalization till the Supreme Court of India. Based on the sentiment expressed by the Prime Minister of India for curbing unnecessary litigation initiated by the Ministry of Defence against its employees and former employees, he was made a part (*gratis*) of a high-level committee of experts constituted by the then defence minister for reducing such litigation by the Ministry of Defence and the defence services in legal, service and pension-related matters, and to strengthen the system of redressal of grievances.

He has attended, lectured and spoken at multiple international and national-level seminars, conferences, universities, institutions and meets, and has written on law, military and public policy for national and international publications. He was a part of the historic 'Yale Draft (Principles)' on military justice, an improvement of the existing United Nations document on the same subject, at a meet at the Yale Law School attended by global jurists and representatives of the United Nations. He was also a part of the drafting committee of the momentous 'Commonwealth Military Justice Principles', popularly known as the 'Stellenbosch Draft'. He has authored five books. He is also a member of the International Society for Military Law and the Law of War, Brussels, and an international fellow of the National Institute of Military Justice, Washington, D.C. He is part of a five-member advisory committee of global experts on military justice recently constituted by the Commonwealth Secretariat, London, and the honorary chief editor of *Forces Law Review*, the first international military law journal.

When not in court, he's probably engrossed in listening to 'Purple Rain' or dissecting pop culture.

Shivani Dasmahapatra is a public policy and communications specialist. Her professional experience of three decades is diverse and ranges from consulting members of Parliament, corporate enterprises, and non-profit organizations to journalism, photography, editing and social media management. Born into a family with three generations in the Indian Army, she has a deep interest in Indian military history.

Currently, as founder trustee of *Lest We Forget India* Foundation, she provides crucial support to the families of Indian Armed Forces personnel. Through the foundation's social media presence, she chronicles India's military history through stories of service and sacrifice of India's soldiers and keeps their legacy alive.

Shivani is a seasoned writer and editor, having worked with *India Today*, *Encyclopedia Britannica* and numerous national publications. She also provides expertise in communications strategy, content development and knowledge product creation to corporates and various organizations.

A passionate advocate, Shivani volunteers for social causes, particularly those focused on child education, women empowerment and animal protection, and is a patron of the Foundation for Media Professionals.

Photography remains Shivani's foremost passion. She continuously explores new techniques and delves into innovative methods to transform her photographs into artworks.

On the rare occasion that you catch her outside of work, it will be undertaking farming in the Himalayan hills in north India or trekking with her family and pet Basset Hound.

ADVANCE PRAISE FOR THE BOOK

'An interesting anthology based on court decisions, which over the years have corrected much of the patriarchal thinking and gender discrimination in the terms and conditions of women serving in our armed and other uniformed forces. As one judgment states, "The battle for gender equality is about confronting the battles of the mind." These battles fought in courts by women for their constitutional rights to bring about positive changes in their terms and condition of service remind me of Captain Liddell Hart's quote, "The only thing harder than getting a new idea into the military mind is to get an old one out." A major lesson from this book for all civil and military organizations is to accept the fast-changing social environment, women's rights and constitutional commitments before legal interventions in courts'—**General V.P. Malik, former chief of the army staff, Indian Army**

'A brilliantly researched and fascinatingly told chronicle. If your heart leaps with pride and joy as mine does every time you see a woman in uniform, this book is essential reading to understand how India got here. Whether you're a student of law, a member of the armed forces or just a proud Indian citizen from any walk of life, Navdeep and Shivani tell a compelling and important story. This is essential reading'—**Barkha Dutt, editor, Mojo Story**

'An excellent explanatory and analytical work that brings together important judgments related to women in the armed forces. It's an unmissable read and irrefutable proof of how inequality affects not only rights but also goes against constitutional guarantees long won. From case to case, the book aims to demonstrate that the woman is "also" capable of fighting "in her defence"'—**Justice Maria Elizabeth Rocha, Superior Military Court of Brazil**

'In ancient Rome, the term "decimation" was used to describe the destruction of one-tenth of an army. Is there a similar term to describe the destruction of half of an army? I suggest there is: gender discrimination. It is a sobering reality that many nations, whether through stereotypes or dogmatic adherence to tradition, still fail to untap the true potential of half of the population of patriotic and able citizens who are willing to do their part for national defence. With this collection of essays, Navdeep Singh and Shivani Dasmahapatra demonstrate the underappreciated synergy between national security and equal protection. These essays will surely challenge shibboleths and inspire new generations of women (and men) in countries all over the world'—**Professor Franklin Rosenblatt, president, National Institute of Military Justice, USA**

IN HER DEFENCE

TEN LANDMARK JUDGMENTS ON WOMEN
IN THE ARMED FORCES

Edited by **NAVDEEP SINGH** and
SHIVANI DASMAHAPATRA

PENGUIN
VEER

An imprint of Penguin Random House

PENGUIN VEER

USA | Canada | UK | Ireland | Australia
New Zealand | India | South Africa | China | Singapore

Penguin Veer is an imprint of the Penguin Random House group of companies
whose addresses can be found at global.penguinrandomhouse.com

Published by Penguin Random House India Pvt. Ltd
4th Floor, Capital Tower 1, MG Road,
Gurugram 122 002, Haryana, India

First published in Penguin Veer by Penguin Random House India 2024

10 9 8 7 6 5 4 3 2

The views and opinions expressed in this book are the authors' own and the
facts are as reported by them, which have been verified to the extent possible,
and the publishers are not in any way liable for the same.

Please note that no part of this book may be used or reproduced in any manner
for the purpose of training artificial intelligence technologies or systems.

ISBN 9780143468295

Typeset in Adobe Caslon Pro by Manipal Technologies Limited, Manipal

Printed at Repro India Limited

www.penguin.co.in

MIX
Paper from
responsible sources
FSC® C047271

This is a legitimate digitally printed version of the book and therefore might not
have certain extra finishing on the cover.

Contents

Foreword

Major Priya Jhingan

It is an honour to pen a foreword for *In Her Defence*, a collection that resonates deeply with both my life's journey and the broader strides made towards equality and justice for women. Having walked the path as the first woman to join the Indian Army, I understand the weight of each such stride and the countless, often invisible, steps that women across generations have taken to carve spaces for themselves within spheres traditionally closed to them.

Empowerment has never been handed to us; it has been attained through sheer resilience and an unyielding belief in justice and equality. Every hard-won right today is built on a foundation of courage, strength and, crucially, the rulings of forward-thinking judges who have reinforced the law with humanity. This book is more than a collection of essays on judgments—it is a tribute to the progress women have made and a road map for the work still ahead. Every ruling captured here stands as a symbol of how justice can both protect and transform lives, redefining what it means to be equal.

In Her Defence takes readers through the pivotal cases that shaped women's rights in India. These aren't just judicial decisions; they are stories of people—women who fought, judges who patiently heard and decided, and the society taking steps forward, however incremental. It is the courage within these cases that has fuelled change, even against the most ingrained norms. These rulings remind us that true justice is built on the values of dignity, respect and equity, upheld by our constitutional courts that understand the stakes at hand.

This book is a testament to the power of justice over prejudice. As you read, I hope you feel as I do—proud, inspired and determined. Let these landmark decisions fuel your own resolve, whether as a reader, an advocate, or simply as someone who believes in equality.

To my colleagues in the defence forces, this book serves as both an anchor and a call to action. Let us lead with integrity, dedication and courage, serving not with any special privileges, but with distinction and purpose. We have a calling to rise on our merit, to prove, through action and excellence, that we deserve every right and responsibility we carry.

Together, let's keep moving forward with strength and pride. This journey is far from over, but each step brings us closer to a future where justice and equality are not goals but realities.

Major Priya Jhingan was the first woman to join the Officers Training Academy, Chennai, when the doors for joining the army were opened to women. She joined the academy with the first batch of twenty-five lady cadets on 21 September 1992, under number LADY CADET-1 / LC-1.

Introduction

For centuries, the tapestry of India's history has been woven with threads of valour and sacrifice, with the armed forces symbolizing the epitome of national pride and protection from external, and often internal, threats. Ten path-breaking essays form the essence of this book, hence, we would not detain readers much with our own pen and just provide a snapshot of what lies inside.

The history of women's participation in the armed forces is rich and multifaceted. It is a story marked by perseverance in the face of adversity—women have continuously sought to challenge the status quo and carve out a space for themselves within this traditionally male-dominated profession. From the earliest days of India's struggle for independence to the present, women have demonstrated their strength and dedication on the battlefield, proving time and again that they are capable of serving their country equally and fearlessly.

The journey of recognizing and affirming the rights of women in the military has been arduous. From 1888, when the Indian Military Nursing Service was formed by the British, to more than a century later, women in the armed forces have faced many challenges. Discriminatory policies and practices have long hindered their progress, denying them opportunities for advancement and relegating them to subordinate roles. Instances of direct and indirect inequity have been ever-present.

Despite these challenges, women have made significant strides in recent decades. In 1992, the Indian Army began inducting women officers in non-medical roles for Short Service Commission. Around the same time, the Indian Air Force and Navy also opened their doors to women in various capacities. This was followed by the permanent commissioning of women officers in select branches such as the Judge Advocate General's department and Army Education Corps in the late 2000s and various other arms/services subsequently. The ongoing process of integrating women into combat roles also marks a significant step forward in acknowledging their capabilities and contributions to national security.

The legal landscape surrounding women in the armed forces has been dynamic. Few arenas within the annals of legal history have witnessed as profound a transformation as the realm of gender equality within the armed forces. This terrain is marked by landmark judgments that have reshaped the landscape of gender inclusivity and representation. It is within this context that we present this comprehensive collection of essays, meticulously curated to illuminate the pivotal judgments that have shaped the trajectory of women's participation in the armed forces of India. Some of these judgments are well known to the public at large, some not as much, interestingly even within the military community, but all of them have one common feature nevertheless—that they are momentous in spirit.

At the heart of this anthology lies a profound commitment to unravelling the intricate legal nuances and sociopolitical implications embedded within each judgment. This transcends mere legal analysis to offer a holistic understanding of the broader implications for gender equality and women empowerment in India.

The essays traverse a rich canvas of legal discourse, offering insightful analyses and critical reflections on some of the most seminal cases to have graced the corridors of justice. These judgments stand as a testament to the judiciary's unwavering dedication to upholding the principles of equality and justice. Furthermore, the essays delve into the finer details of important cases and their background, each representing a significant milestone in the quest for gender inclusivity and recognition within the armed forces. As is the case in many a dictum in constitutional law, some of the judgments aid in lifting the veil over tacit discrimination that is not directly discernible to a common citizen, and the authors explain the minutiae in layperson terms.

As editors, it is our fervent belief that this anthology will serve as a beacon of knowledge and insight for scholars, legal practitioners, policymakers, lawyers and general readers alike. By chronicling the evolution of jurisprudence surrounding women in the armed forces, we hope to inspire dialogue, foster understanding and catalyse transformative change within the realms of law and society. We also hope that the voice of change emerges from within the forces, rather than being brought in through judicial intervention every time. The *nari shakti* in the uniformed forces has been ushered by our courts, while in an ideal society in tune with the times, progressive change should have organically emanated from within.

It would be worthwhile to explain the layout and the methodology of the book here. The essays are sequentially arranged based on the spirit of the subject and not by date or any other criterion.

As editors, we have not altered the spirit of the expression of the authors so as to retain the originality and to avoid over-standardization. The terminology 'armed forces' includes not just the defence services but also the Central Armed Police Forces (CAPF)—though it would definitely be interesting to note, and it goes to their credit, that the forces under the Ministry of Home Affairs have been much more welcoming to women with an openness to putting progressive policies into place. The resistance towards granting permanence to women in uniformed professions is apparent in many of these essays. It is also worth noticing the overwhelming number of judgments revolving around marriage, and even pregnancy—the very source of human existence.

We hope you enjoy reading this book, as much as we enjoyed compiling and editing it.

We extend our sincere gratitude to each of the contributors who dedicated their time, expertise and passion to write essays for this book. Going much beyond the subject, your thoughtful insights and perspectives have enriched our understanding of all forms of direct and indirect discrimination at the workplace. We are deeply grateful for your invaluable contributions.

We would also like to express heartfelt appreciation to our respective families for their unwavering support throughout the journey of bringing this book to fruition.

We would also thank Akanksha Duvedi, who assisted us in formulating our thoughts at the initial stages of the project, and Ananya Sharma in her important capacity of being a thorough editorial sounding board.

Gratitude also to Anushree Kaushal, Gurveen Chadha and Saba Nehal of Penguin Random House India. Without their vital support, this book would not have been possible.

We dedicate this book to all the women in uniform— the trailblazers and pioneers. You stand as beacons of hope, breaking barriers and challenging stereotypes with every step you take. You have not only carved out a space for yourselves but have also paved the way for future generations of women to follow in your footsteps. Your presence in the forces is a symbol of progress as well as empowerment, a reminder that equality knows no bounds. This book is a tribute to your courage, your strength and your indomitable spirit. May it serve as a testament to your legacy and a source of inspiration for the times to come.

Most significantly, before we sign off, we recognize and salute the profound impact of the judiciary on societal transformation. The landmark judgments discussed in this book exemplify just one facet of the transformative power of the judicial system in upholding the constitutional right to equality. And, of course, this book and this subject would not exist but for our constitutional courts.

Sincerely,
Navdeep Singh and Shivani Dasmahapatra

1

A Judicially Aided
Leap Towards Equality

Justice A.K. Patnaik

Secretary, Ministry of Defence v. Babita Puniya

If society holds strong beliefs about gender roles – that men are socially dominant, physically powerful and the breadwinners of the family and that women are weak and physically submissive, and primarily caretakers confined to a domestic atmosphere – it is unlikely that there would be a change in mindsets.

—The Supreme Court of India in *Secretary, Ministry of Defence v. Babita Puniya*

The inherent doubt on a woman's capability in the battlefield is not new, this age-old scepticism has endured through history. Yet, the indomitable spirit of Lakshmibai Newalkar, the valiant Rani of Jhansi, shattered these misconceptions as she fearlessly battled

British forces and fell in June 1858 during the First War of Independence.

The Supreme Court's decision in the *Babita Puniya* case pushes the frontiers of law forward. It recognizes and addresses historical biases and strives to pave the way for a more inclusive and equitable future in the realm of women's participation in the armed forces.

The Constitution of India was adopted on 26 November 1949, and it came into force on 26 January 1950. It was provided in Article 14 of our Constitution that the State shall not deny to any person equality before law or the equal protection of the laws within the territory of India. Article 15 (1) of the Constitution of India further provided that the State shall not discriminate against any citizen on the grounds only of sex. In Article 16 (1) of the Constitution of India, equality of opportunity for all citizens in the matters relating to employment or appointment to any office under the State was guaranteed. These provisions in the Constitution of India were made to ensure that no citizen, including women, was discriminated against by the State while making laws and in providing employment. Article 33 of the Constitution of India, however, conferred the power on the Parliament to determine the extent to which any fundamental rights could be restricted or abrogated in their application to the members of the armed forces, so as to ensure the proper discharge of their duties and the maintenance of discipline among them.

It was purportedly in exercising this power that the Parliament provided—in Section 12 of the Army Act, 1950:

12. Ineligibility of females for enrolment or employment.

No female shall be eligible for enrolment or employment in the regular Army, except in such corps, department, branch or other body forming part of, or attached to any portion of, the regular Army as the Central Government may, by notification in the Official Gazette, specify in this behalf.

Thus, this section restricted the fundamental rights of women citizens to equal opportunity of employment in the regular army available under Articles 14, 15 and 16 of the Constitution of India. It also conferred power on the Central government to decide the corps, department, branch or other body forming of, or attached to any portion of, the regular army in which women citizens could be employed.

The legend of Rani of Jhansi notwithstanding, it took more than forty years for the Central government to decide that women will be eligible for appointment in the specific branches or cadres of the army. By notification dated 30 January 1992, women became eligible to become officers in the Army Postal Service, Judge Advocate General's Department, Army Education Corps and some branches of the Army Ordnance Corps and Army Service Corps. Thereafter, by notification dated 31 December 1992, women became eligible for commission in the Corps of Signals, Intelligence Corps, Corps of Engineers, Corps of Electrical and Mechanical Engineering and in the Regiment of the Artillery. Initially commissioned only for a period of five years, by subsequent notifications, the tenure of women officers in the army was extended up to fourteen years. The Short Service Commission (SSC) scheme for women officers was known as the Women Special Entry Scheme.[1]

In February 2003, Babita Puniya, an advocate, filed a writ petition in the Delhi High Court as a Public Interest Litigation (PIL) for protecting the rights of some women army officers who were selected and appointed as SSC officers commencing 1995–96. While the writ petition was pending before the Delhi High Court, two circulars were issued on 20 July 2006 conveying the sanction of the President of India for granting SSC, both on the technical and non-technical side, to women officers. Major Leena Gurav, a serving officer, challenged the terms and conditions imposed by the circulars of July 2006 and sought the grant of Permanent Commission (PC) for women officers in a writ petition before the Delhi High Court. On 26 September 2008, the Ministry of Defence issued a circular emphasizing the grant of PC prospectively to SSC women officers in Judge Advocate General's Department and Army Education Corps. This circular was also challenged before the Delhi High Court by Major Sandhya Yadav and others on the ground that it granted PC only prospectively and was restricted to certain specified cadres.

A division bench of the Delhi High Court delivered its judgment on 12 March 2010[2] wherein it held that, being a policy decision, the challenge to absorption in frontline combat branches that were not open for recruitment of women officers could not be sustained. The Delhi High Court, however, observed that if the SSC officers had performed equally well in their task, such that the Central government had extended the period of said commission more than once, it would be a gross violation of Articles 14, 16 and 21 of the Constitution to accept a situation where such women officers were deprived of PC, while male officers were granted the opportunity to opt for the same. The court further held that a PC carries with it certain privileges of rank, including pension, and women officers who have served well in the armed forces of the country for fourteen years, should not be deprived of these benefit on the ground that they chose to accept the SSC and, by implication, decided to go out of service on its completion as prescribed from time to time. The division bench further asserted that if the Central government had decided to extend PC prospectively, it should extend consideration for PC to SSC officers in service or those who retired during the petition's pendency. Consequently, the Delhi High Court issued directives for considering SSC women officers for PC, along with consequential benefits.

The Union of India challenged the judgment of the Delhi High Court before the Supreme Court. On 11 November 2011, the Supreme Court issued a notice and granted the Central government's request for an adjournment. This was done to allow a High Powered Committee, formed by the Union of India, to review the issue of granting PC to SSC women officers. It also gave time for the Chiefs of Staff Committee and the Ministry of

Defence to review the committee's report. On 2 September 2011, the Supreme Court clarified in its order that the operation of the judgment of the Delhi High Court was not stayed at all, and only the action of contempt initiated by the original writ petitioners before the high court had been stayed.

During the pendency of the appeal before the Supreme Court, the Central government issued a communication on 25 February 2019 granting PC to SSC women officers in eight branches in the Indian Army—namely Signals, Engineers, Army Aviation, Army Air Defence, Electronics and Mechanical Engineers, Army Service Corps, Army Ordnance Corps, and Intelligence, in addition to the existing two streams of Judge Advocate General and Army Education Corps. This communication further stipulated that:

i.   Women officers will continue to be commissioned in the above-mentioned ten arms/services as earlier with no change in their tenure of SSC engagement.

ii. On the completion of three years, and before completing four years of commissioned service, they will be required to exercise an option for the grant of PC and the choice of specialization.

iii. SSC women officers will be considered for the grant of PC based on the availability of vacancies and subject to willingness, suitability, performance, medical fitness and competitive merit.

iv. On the grant of PC, women officers will be employed 'in various staff appointments only' in accordance with their qualifications, professional experience, specialization, if any, and organizational requirements.

v. While women officers who are granted PC will continue to be a part of their parent arm/service, 'they would serve on staff appointments only' both within the parent arm/service and in other fields of specialization.

vi. Further career progression in selected ranks will be within the existing authorized strength of officers in the army and no additional select rank[3] vacancies will be created.

vii. Women officers who fail to exercise the option for PC will be governed by the terms and conditions under which they were commissioned.

viii. The policy would come into effect prospectively from the date of the issuance of the letter.[4]

The Supreme Court bench comprising Justices D.Y. Chandrachud and Ajay Rastogi considered the arguments made on behalf of the Ministry of Defence and those made by the respondents (the petitioners before the high court and other affected parties), and held in its judgment dated 17 February 2020 titled *Secretary, Ministry of Defence v. Babita Puniya & Ors*[5] that the policy decision of the Union government in the policy circular dated 25 February 2019 was a recognition of the right of women officers to equality of opportunity and enforces the right against discrimination on the ground of sex in Article 15 (1) of the Constitution of India as well as the right to equal opportunity to all citizens in matters of public employment under Article 16 (1) of the Constitution. These fundamental rights are recognized in all of the ten streams of service in the Army where women were allowed to serve, the court observed. It was also noted that this decision of the Union government to extend the grant of PC to women recognized that physiological features of a woman have no significance to an equal entitlement under the Constitution. The Supreme Court observed that it was conscious of the limitation of national security and policy for which engagement of women in the combat arms had been specifically held to be a matter of policy by the judgment of the Delhi High Court. Strong observations were also made by the court on the stereotypical notions of womanhood and their physiological qualities as submitted by the government before the court. The court observed thus:

> Seventy years after the birth of a postcolonial independent state, there is still a need for change in attitudes and mindsets to recognize the commitment to the values of the Constitution. This is evident from the submissions which were placed as a part of the record of this court . . . The submissions advanced in the note tendered to this court are based on sex stereotypes premised on assumptions about socially ascribed roles of gender which discriminate against women. Underlying the statement that it is a 'greater challenge' for women officers to meet the hazards of service 'owing to their prolonged absence during pregnancy, motherhood and

domestic obligations towards their children and families'
is a strong stereotype which assumes that domestic
obligations rest solely on women.[6]

The Supreme Court found that the proposal of the Union
government in its policy circular dated 25 February 2019
made a distinction between women officers who have
been in service for a period less than fourteen years, and
those who have been in service for a period more than
fourteen years. The proposal of the Union government
envisaged that only those women officers with less than
fourteen years of service would be considered for the
grant of PC. The proposal also provided that women
officers with more than fourteen years of service, but less
than twenty years of service would continue until they
attain pensionable service of twenty years. The Supreme
Court held that there was a fundamental fallacy in
this distinction between women officers with less than
fourteen years of service, those with service between
fourteen to twenty years, and those above twenty years.
This situation of women officers with service above
fourteen years was because of the failure of the Union
government to comply with the directions of the Delhi
High Court in the judgment dated 12 March 2010, which
the Supreme Court had refused to stay in its order dated
2 September 2011. The Supreme Court, therefore, did
not see any reason or justification to deprive SSC women
officers for the grant of PC on the ground that they had
crossed fourteen years of service. Accordingly, the court

held that the policy decision of the Union of India will apply to all SSC officers who were in service at the time of the judgment of the Supreme Court, irrespective of their length of the service.

The Supreme Court also found that in the policy decision of the Union of India dated 25 February 2019, women were made eligible for PC only for staff appointments and that an absolute bar on women seeking criteria[7] or command[8] appointments would be violative of the guarantee of equality under Article 14 of the Constitution. The Supreme Court also observed that restricting women SSC officers to only staff appointments does not fulfil the purpose of providing PC as a means of career advancement in the army. It also emphasized that it was for the competent authority to consider whether a particular candidate should or should not be granted a criteria or command assignment, having regard to the exigencies of service, performance and organizational requirements. However, the court stated that women should not be excluded from such opportunities based on a policy decision.

While upholding the judgment of the Delhi High Court to the extent that the claim of absorption in areas of operation not open for recruitment of women officers cannot be sustained being a policy decision, the Supreme Court endorsed the grant of PC to women and also the policy decision of the Union of India contained in the policy circular dated 25 February 2019, subject to the following as recorded in the judgment:

i.   All serving women officers on SSC shall be considered for the grant of PC irrespective of any of them having crossed fourteen years or, as the case may be, twenty years of service.

ii. The option shall be granted to all women presently in service as SSC officers.

iii. Women officers on SSC with more than fourteen years of service, who do not opt for being considered for the grant of the PC, will be entitled to continue in service until they attain twenty years of pensionable service.

iv. As a one-time measure, the benefit of continuing in service until the attainment of pensionable service shall also apply to all the existing SSC officers with more than fourteen years of service, who are not appointed on PC.

v.   The expression 'in various staff appointments only' in Para 5 and 'on staff appointments only' in Para 6 of the circular dated 25 February 2019 shall not be enforced.

vi. SSC women officers with over twenty years of service, who are not granted PC shall retire on pension in terms of the policy decision.

vii. At the stage of opting for the grant of PC, all the choices for specialization shall be available to women officers on the same terms as for the male SSC officers. Women SSC officers shall be entitled to exercise their options for being considered for the grant of PC on the same terms as their male counterparts.[9]

The Supreme Court further held that SSC officers, who are granted PC in pursuance of the above directions will be entitled to all consequences and benefits including promotion and financial benefits. These benefits will also be made available to those officers in service or those who had moved the Delhi High Court by filing the writ petitions and those who had retired during the course of the pendency of the appeals before the Supreme Court.

The judgment in *Babita Puniya* is a long leap forward for women in India who aspire to serve in the army. Interestingly, after the Delhi High Court had pronounced the judgment, the Indian Air Force had materially complied with the dictum but the same was not given proper effect by the Indian Army and the Indian Navy, leading to further complications and litigation. The Parliament has amended the Constitution to provide one-third of the seats in the Lok Sabha and the state assemblies after noticing that women were no less than men in their ability to represent their constituencies. The same sentiment must emanate from within the defence services, rather than through judicial intervention.

I have no doubt that a day will come when the Parliament will repeal Section 12 of the Army Act, 1950 altogether and give full effect to the fundamental right to equality of opportunity to women guaranteed by Articles 14, 15 and 16 of the Constitution of India in the defence forces. It will definitely require a fundamental change in the mindset of the Indian society towards women. Indeed, that would be the ultimate tribute by modern India to Rani of Jhansi.

2

A Footnote in the Battle for Equality?

Justice Rajive Bhalla

Union of India v. Lieutenant Commander
Annie Nagaraja

Annie Nagaraja's judgment[1] will go down in judicial history as a battle in the war for equality that is waged daily, but as I have been entrusted with the task of analysing the judgment of the Supreme Court in a case where seventeen brave women decided to take on the establishment's denial of Permanent Commission (PC)[2] to them in the navy, I would commence by stating that the ground for denial, simply put, was that they were women.

Two eminent judges of the Supreme Court of India, Dr D.Y. Chandrachud, Chief Justice of India, and Justice Ajay Rastogi, preceded by judges of the Delhi High Court and members of the Armed Forces Tribunal, held that the government was wrong in denying PC in the navy on the sole ground that the candidates, though eligible, were women.

The judgment is a comforting assurance that though women's rights may be in retreat in other democracies—the recent reversal of *Roe v. Wade*[3] is a case in point—such mindset shall not visit our shores. It is an assurance that we shall continue in our quest to achieve equality in all spheres.

The battle for gender equality is about confronting the battles of the mind.

These are words employed in this judgment. The judgment, of course, is in line with a host of other dicta by the Supreme Court setting aside age-old practices of gender discrimination prohibiting women from employment conditions at par with men, and in this case, denying PC to women officers in the Indian Navy. A practice, to use a turn of phrase, that has now found its right place at the bottom of the sea.

Seventeen Short Service Commissioned (SSC)[4] women officers serving in various branches of the Indian Navy were denied PC on the basis of a communication issued by the Ministry of Defence on 26 September 2008. The ministry, however, granted PC to those who would join the navy after the said date. The officers approached the Delhi High Court and the Armed Forces Tribunal asserting that the communication issued by the Ministry of Defence, in the purported exercise of power under Sec 9(2) of the Navy Act, deprived them of their right to a PC despite notifications and regulations to the contrary issued by the ministry. The communication, therefore, could not divest them of their vested rights.

The Delhi High Court and the Armed Force Tribunal in their separate opinions in 2015 held that as prior notifications and regulations had opened up regular service to SSC officers, whether men or women, serving women officers could not be denied a PC.

The Union of India challenged these judgments before the Supreme Court in 2015 primarily on the ground that unlike the army and the air force, the navy has a distinctive feature that requires officers to serve on ships. To fortify this objection, one of the facts pressed into service was, and this is not in jest, that 'there is an absence of toilet facilities for women' onboard Indian Navy ships. The government also pointed out that women have always been excluded from sea-going branches with the exception of the logistics cadre. The ministry was therefore right in denying PC to SSC women officers in the navy. It was also argued that the 2008 guidelines were enacted to implement the earlier policy decisions and as no rights accrued to SSC women officers on the basis of policy notified on 25 February 1999—the ministry had not committed any error. The government invoked Article 33 of the Constitution of India concerning restriction of fundamental rights and its right to decide when, where and how women would serve in the Indian Navy. It sought to argue that notifications dated 20 December 1991, 1 July 1992, 16 July 1998 and 25 February 1999, which had cleared the path for women to serve as permanent officers in all branches of the Indian Navy subject to their fulfilling the prescribed criteria in accordance with Regulation 203 of Chapter IX of the 1963 Regulations, were not applicable. The government persisted in its argument that the principle of equality has been adhered to by allowing women to serve in the navy, but the offer of a PC was a practical impossibility as women were unsuited to serve on ships at the high seas.

A reading of the arguments raises a perplexing question—why did a progressive democracy like India defer to a regressive mindset prohibiting women officers from PC? The judgment, however, rejects this mindset as it forcefully repels the government's contentions.

The Judgment

The judgment can be broadly divided into three distinct parts: the soul of the judgment; the interpretation of the Navy Act, notifications, letters, regulations, etc.; and the directions.

The Soul:

The words 'no woman shall be eligible' for appointment in the navy or the Indian Naval Reserve Forces, the cause for much misery to serving women SSC officers, should have had no place in an enlightened society, but despite opposition was included in Section 9(2) of the Navy Act is by itself an interesting fact.

The Navy Bill was placed before a joint committee of the Parliament in November 1957. Four members of the committee, T.C.N. Menon, K.K. Warior, V.K. Dhage and V. Prasad Rao recorded an important dissent as follows:

> An important provision of the Bill is the one which excludes women from the right of joining the Indian Navy. It will be superfluous if we record in detail the courage and capacity shown by the women of India in the past and especially during our glorious freedom struggle. In almost all countries women have proved themselves to be equal to men if not more and today there is no sphere of life nor is there any kind of work where women cannot compete with men. Moreover, we feel that the admission of women into our armed services will, to a very large extent, have a salutary and welcome effect upon the outlook and morale of our fighting men. This injustice done to our women should be removed and we recommend that the clause which prohibits women from joining the navy be removed.[5]

An interesting but significant piece of trivia, that the judgment notices where four dissenting Parliamentarians tried to warn the Parliament about the injustice of depriving women of service in the navy by pointing out that there is no sphere in life where women cannot compete with men. A paragraph from the judgment that tends to resonate this opinion requires reproduction:

The battle for gender equality is about confronting the battles of the mind. History is replete with examples where women have been denied their just entitlements under law and the right to fair and equal treatment in the workplace. In the context of the Armed Forces, specious reasons have been advanced by decision makers and administrators. They range from physiology, motherhood and physical attributes to the male-dominated hierarchies. A hundred and one excuses are no answer to the constitutional entitlement to dignity, which attaches to every individual irrespective of gender, to fair and equal conditions of work and to a level playing field. A level playing field ensures that women have the opportunity to overcome their histories of discrimination with the surest of responses based on their competence, ability and performance.[6]

A precise and pithy rejection of the stand of the State to retain injustice.

Another paragraph in the judgment citing the dicta in *Ministry of Defence v. Babita Puniya* that carries the opinion forward and illustrates the misogynist mindset, that women are best locked up at home with the kitchen as their area of influence, is:

The submissions advanced in the note tendered to this court are based on sex stereotypes premised on assumptions about socially ascribed roles of gender which discriminate against women. Underlying the statement that it is a greater challenge for women officers to meet the hazards of service owing to their prolonged absence during pregnancy, motherhood and domestic obligations towards their children and families is a strong stereotype which assumes that domestic obligations rest solely on women. Reliance on the inherent physiological differences between men and women rests in a deeply entrenched stereotypical and constitutionally flawed notion that women are the weaker sex and may not undertake tasks that are too arduous for them.

Arguments founded on the physical strengths and weaknesses of men and women and on assumptions about women in the social context of marriage and family do not constitute a constitutionally valid basis for denying equal opportunity to women officers.[7]

The soul of the judgment is thus the right of women to be treated equally and resonates as an article of faith that owes its origin to the rights of women as human beings and not just to the Constitution of India. The judgment thereafter proceeds to examine the Act and the regulations.

The Interpretation:

After considering the statutory framework of the Navy Act, Article 33 of the Constitution, various notifications and regulations, the Supreme Court minced no words in repelling the Union of India's arguments that women are unsuited for service on the high seas. The Supreme Court held that the statutory bar to the engagement or involvement of women in the Indian Navy had been lifted to the extent set out in the notifications issued by the Union government on 9 October 1990 to 16 November 1998 issued under Section 9(2) of the 1957 Act. The policy decision of the Union government dated 25 February 1999 set out the terms and conditions of service of SSC officers, including women, in regard to grant of PC, governed by Regulation 203, Chapter IX, Part III of the 1963 Regulations. The policy letter dated 26 September 2008, which sought to ignore the policy of 1999 by making PC prospective and restricting its application to specified cadres and branches, was declared invalid.

The attempt to turn the clock back by disregarding these notifications was held to be illegal and emphatically declared not to apply to women officers of the navy. The judgment also took note of Article 33 of the Constitution of India which entrusts to the Parliament the right to determine the extent to which rights conferred by Part III of the Constitution can be restricted in their application to members of the armed forces 'so as to ensure the proper discharge of the duties and maintenance of discipline amongst them', relied on to buttress the government's arguments. After referring to the judgments in *Prithi Pal Singh Bedi v. Union of India* (1982) 3 SCC 140, *R Viswan v. Union of India* (1983) 3 SCC 401, *Union of India v. LD Balam Singh* (2002) 9 SCC 73, the Supreme Court held in a forceful validation of the law of equality that notifications dated 9 October 1991 and 6 November 1998 did not restrict the appointment or enrolment of women to only SSC, as they stipulate that women shall be eligible for appointment as officers in the Indian Navy in the branches specified. The Supreme Court relied upon the doctrine of legitimate expectation extending it to the field of equality of women, a significant enunciation of the law. It was also observed that:

The course of the evolution of policy from 9 October 1991 clearly indicates a legitimate expectation on part of the SSC officers (both men and women) of being governed by the provisions of Regulation 203 being considered for the grant of PCs. The Navy Regulations, when they were originally drafted in 1963, did not contemplate the induction of women. For this reason, Regulations 122(2), 124(2) and 126(2) spoke of only unmarried males being eligible for induction on SSC. The Regulations being subservient to statute, incorporated restrictions which comported with the provisions of Section 9(2). However, what Section 9(2) envisages is that the restrictions on the enrolment or appointment of women in branches or departments of the Indian Navy would be lifted upon the issuance of a notification by the Union Government sanctioning the entry of women officers, subject to the conditions which may be specified. Both in the notifications dated 9 October 1991 and 6 November 1998, the Union Government lifted the statutory bar in exercise of its enabling power under Section 9(2) by allowing for the entry for women as officers in the Indian Navy in stipulated branches. Once the statutory bar stood lifted, the appointment of SSC officers, both men and women on PCs would be governed uniformly by the provisions of Regulation 203. This was made abundantly clear by the policy letter dated 25 February 1999 which was issued in compliance with the legal regime. The grant of PCs to SSC men and women officers aligned with the provisions of Regulation 203 which plainly is a matter of law. Thus, the contention urged by Mr Sanjay Jain, learned Additional Solicitor General that the communication dated 25 February 1999 was merely anticipatory in nature and that the entitlement to be considered for the grant of PCs would have to await a further policy, which came into being on 26 September 2008 cannot be accepted. The communication dated 25 February 1999 of the MoD had the sanction of the President and consequently cannot be disregarded as suggested in the arguments urged by the Union of India in these proceedings.[8]

The judgment, in no uncertain terms, dealt a blow to the offending words used in Section 9(2) prohibiting women from the service in the navy by holding that the Ministry of Defence's decision dated 26 September 2008 was invalid.

The Supreme Court has also held that the submission by the Union was based upon a deeply entrenched stereotype that had already been rejected in *Ministry of*

Defence v. Babita Puniya.[9] This is best summed up with the following quote from the judgment:

> Quite apart from the policy letter dated 25 February 1999, the contention that certain sea-going duties are ill-suited to women officers is premised on sex stereotypes that male officers are more suited to certain duties by virtue of the physiological characteristics. As this Court has noted in Babita Puniya, arguments founded on the physical strengths and weaknesses of men and women do not constitute a constitutionally valid basis for denying equal opportunity to women officers. To accept the contention urged by the ASG would be to approve the socially ascribed gender roles which a commitment to equal worth and dignity of every individual belies.[10]

Babita Puniya, in any case, is also discussed in detail in this book.

The Directions:

After declaring that women have a right to serve as PC officers, the court issued directions in the following terms. The reason for reproducing these directions is that they traverse areas that are exclusively reserved for the executive, but in the exercise of the plenary jurisdiction, the court was bound to intervene to protect the rights of women serving in the navy:

(i)   The statutory bar on the engagement or enrolment of women in the Indian Navy has been lifted to the extent envisaged in the notifications issued by the Union Government on 9 October 1991 and 6 November 1998 under Section 9(2) of the 1957 Act;

(ii) By and as a result of the policy decision of the Union Government in the Ministry of Defence dated 25 February 1999, the terms and conditions of service of SSC officers, including women in regard to the grant of PC are governed by Regulation 203, Chapter IX, Part III of the 1963 Regulations;

(iii) The stipulation in the policy letter dated 26 September 2008 making it prospective and restricting its application to specified cadres/branches of the Indian Navy shall not be enforced;

(iv) The provisions of the implementation guidelines dated 3 December 2008, to the extent that they are made prospective and restricted to specified cadres are quashed and set aside;

(v)   All SSC officers in the Education, Law and Logistics cadres who are presently in service shall be considered for the grant of PC. The right to be considered for the grant of PC arises from the policy letter dated 25 February 1999 read with Regulation 203 of Chapter IX Part III of the 1963 Regulations. SSC women officers in the batch of cases before the high court and the AFT, who are presently in service shall be considered for the grant of PCs on the basis of the vacancy position as on the date of judgments of the Delhi High Court and the AFT or as it presently stands, whichever is higher;

(vi) The period of service after which women SSC officers shall be entitled to submit applications for the grant of PC shall be the same as their male counterparts;

(vii) The applications of the serving officers for the grant of PC shall be considered on the basis of the norms contained in Regulation 203 namely: (i) availability of vacancies in the stabilized cadre at the material time; (ii) determination of suitability; and (iii) recommendation of the Chief of the Naval Staff. Their empanelment shall be based on inter se merit evaluated on the ACRs of the officers under consideration, subject to the availability of vacancies;

(viii) SSC officers who are found suitable for the grant of PC shall be entitled to all consequential benefits including arrears of pay, promotions and retiral benefits as and when due;

(ix) Women SSC officers of the ATC cadre in *Annie Nagaraja*'s case are not entitled to consideration for the grant of PC since neither men nor women SSC officers are considered for the grant of PC and there is no direct induction of men officers to PC. In exercise of the power conferred by Article 142 of the Constitution, we direct that as a one-time measure, SSC officers in the ATC cadre in *Annie Nagaraja*'s case shall be entitled to pensionary benefits. SSC officers in the ATC cadre in *Priya Khurana*'s case, being inducted in pursuance of the specific representation contained in the advertisements pursuant to which they were inducted, shall be considered for the grant of PC in accordance with directions (v) and (vi) above;

(x) All SSC women officers who were denied consideration for the grant of PC on the ground that they were inducted prior to the issuance of the letter dated 26 September 2008 and who are not presently in service shall be deemed, as a one-time measure, to have completed substantive pensionable service. Their pensionary benefits shall be computed and released on this basis. No arrears of salary shall be payable for the period after release from service;

(xi) As a one-time measure, all SSC women officers who were before the high court and the AFT who are not granted PCs shall be deemed to have completed substantive qualifying service for the grant of pension and shall be entitled to all consequential benefits; and

(xii) Respondents two to six in the Civil Appeals arising out of Special Leave Petition (C) Nos 30791-96 of 2015, namely Commander R. Prasanna, Commander Puja Chhabra, Commander Saroj Kumar, Commander Sumita Balooni and Commander E. Prasanna shall be entitled, in addition to the grant of pensionary benefits, as a

one-time measure, to compensation quantified at
₹25 lakhs each.[11]

The case, as presented, underscores the intricate play
between policy decisions and individual rights. It reinforces
the principle that justice is neither a monolith nor a one-
size-fits-all concept but requires a compassionate, context-
aware response, particularly when addressing the unique
challenges faced by women in traditionally male-dominated
spheres.

These directions not only validate the right of
women to serve as PC officers in the Indian Navy but
also reshape the landscape of gender equality within the
armed forces. The significance of these directions extends
beyond the legal realm. They represent a pioneering step
towards dismantling systemic gender biases and fostering
a more inclusive and equitable environment and reflect
a commitment to rectifying historical injustices. In the
context of the broader fight against inequality, these serve
as a poignant reminder of the delicate balance required in
crafting policies that can either uplift or oppress.

The directions are path-breaking in their direct,
salutary effect on future challenges to inequality. The facts
of this case, and the resultant judgment, are a lesson for
our times. Tread carefully while depriving people of their
rights for not everyone can fight the war.

3

Discrimination, We See You

Rajshekhar Rao

Lt Col Nitisha v. Union of India

'Long years ago, we made a tryst with destiny, and now the time comes when we shall redeem our pledge, not wholly or in full measure, but very substantially.'

This short but significant excerpt from Pandit Nehru's speech[1] to the Constituent Assembly, on the eve of India's independence, remains ever relevant and is recalled each time a glass ceiling is broken with respect to religion, sex, gender, caste or class. It serves as a reminder of the adage that 'the more things change, the more they stay the same'. While some things have changed for the better, and we have progressed as a nation on many fronts, there are 'miles to go before (we) sleep'.[2]

The issue of Permanent Commissions (PC) to women in the armed forces is one such instance. Despite women having been part of the Indian Army for over a century and being permanently commissioned into the Army Medical Corps and the Army Dental Corps since 1958, it was only made possible with judicial intervention and that too, after a litigation spanning nearly two decades.

Winds of Change

Historically, barring the Medical, Dental and Nursing Services, women officers were only engaged on Short Service Commissions (SSC) in certain branches of the Indian Army, for a duration of five years, under the Women Special Entry Scheme (Officers). Over time, this was extended into an SSC tenure capped at fourteen years of service. In this backdrop, a PIL titled *Babita Puniya v. Ministry of Defence*[3] was filed before the Delhi High Court in 2003 by Ms Puniya, a practising advocate, who challenged the denial of PC to Women SSC Officers as being discriminatory and violative of the right to equality guaranteed by Article 14 of the Constitution of India. This was followed by a batch of other petitions seeking similar reliefs.

These petitions culminated in a judgment dated 12 March 2010 passed by the Delhi High Court which held that the respondents could not have denied grant of PC to Women SSC Officers who were granted extensions and directed that they be placed on par with their male counterparts along with all consequential promotions and benefits.

Although the 2010 decision was challenged by the Union government before the Supreme Court in 2011, the Ministry of Defence issued a policy circular, dated 25 February 2019, that paved the way for women to be considered for a grant of PC, *albeit* prospectively. This was the first active step taken by the government to permit the commission and engagement of women on a permanent basis into eight arms and services, in addition to the Judge Advocate General and Army Education Corps branches, which were included in the ambit of PC in 2008.

By its judgment in *Secretary, Ministry of Defence v. Babita Puniya*,[4] the Supreme Court proceeded to affirm the decision of the Delhi High Court, albeit with some modifications. The Supreme Court observed that the policy circular dated 25 February 2019 had to be understood as a decision of the government that enforced 'the fundamental right of women to seek access to public appointment and to equality of opportunity in matters of engagement relating to the Army'[5] and that the decision of the government to grant PC to Women SSC officers across all ten streams was 'a step forward in recognizing and realizing the right of women to equality of opportunity in the Army' and that it marked 'a step towards realizing the fundamental constitutional commitment to the equality and dignity of women'.[6] The court also observed that the impugned policy decision could not have placed a blanket restriction over women seeking criteria or command appointments, as it fell foul of the guarantee of equality under Article 14 of the Indian Constitution.

The Aftermath of Babita Punyia

In furtherance of the above, the Union government set up a Special Selection Board (SSB) for the screening, evaluation and consideration of 615 Women SSC Officers for grant of PC into the ten permitted arms/ services in the army. The basis of selection under the existing policy regarding PC was sought to be applied uniformly to all officers, irrespective of sex. This screening process involved the computation of scores of officers on a consideration of aspects such as annual confidential reports (ACRs), honours and awards, performance on courses, recommendations for PC, disciplinary awards, and strong and weak points, etc. After comparing the marks of 615 women candidates against the lowest-scoring male candidate, 422 officers were deemed eligible for consideration of the grant of PC on the basis of merit, subject to them meeting the selection criteria. While fifty-seven officers opted out of the selection process, a total of 277 out of the remaining 365 officers were granted PC by the SSB.

Aggrieved by the manner in which the process was implemented, a group of eighty-six petitioners challenged the selection process directly before the Supreme Court under Article 32 of the Constitution in a petition captioned *Lt Col Nitisha & Ors v. Union of India & Ors.*[7]

Primary Grounds for Challenge and What Was Sought from the Court

The contentions of the petitioners before the Supreme Court can be summarized as follows:

a) *Firstly*, it was contended that the medical criteria that was required to be met by women was arbitrary and unjustified as it was essentially a mechanical reproduction of the criteria set for men. The petitioners submitted that it was discriminatory to expect women to meet the standards set for men, who were anywhere between their fifth to tenth year of service. The women officers pointed out that their bodies had undergone various physiological changes with the passage of time. The disadvantage was particularly apparent in the backdrop of the petitioners having to wait for a significant period of time to even submit to a medical examination due to the impending litigation. Therefore, to expect women officers, who, at the time of consideration, would be in the age group of forty-five to fifty years, to conform to the medical standards set for a male officer in the group of twenty-five to thirty years would be an insurmountable task, particularly when there was going to be no material change in the nature or profile of their service.

b) *Second*, the rationale behind the grading process of the petitioners in their respective ACRs was seriously questioned, owing to the flaws in the way they were prepared for women SSC officers. The petitioners submitted that relying on an evaluation tool that had never considered a situation where women would be considered for a grant of PC was antithetical to the objective of providing the petitioners a fair opportunity. Most ACR report forms had been filled in a perfunctory manner—columns pertaining to the medical fitness of candidates were left blank, and there were no remarks or recommendations given in the columns relating to consideration of grant of PC to the petitioners. Furthermore, since women were only considered for SSC till 2019, any laurels or qualifications attained after the tenth year of service were not recorded in their ACRs.

c) *Third*, the total score obtained by each women officer was compared with the lowest-scoring male candidate, prior to competing on inter se merit with the other candidates, so as to determine the qualification of the woman officer for a grant of PC. Therefore, the requirement for the petitioners to meet an artificial and external benchmark, which is otherwise not the case for men, was discriminatory.

d) *Fourth*, the petitioners were not informed of the vacancies available in each batch within the applicable arm/service for which they would be considered. This resulted in them being denied the right to make an informed choice.

Defence of the Union Government

The fulcrum of the government's case was that the issue of granting PC to women officers was a matter of policy and that courts should not interfere in such matters. Emphasizing the various steps taken to improve representation and opportunities afforded to women in the Indian Army, the Union government submitted the following in response to the arguments advanced by the petitioners:

a) *First*, the Indian Army contended that the medical criteria set out for the evaluation of the candidates was an 'intrinsic and inseparable' part of the process, which was applicable to men and women alike. It was explained to the court that it was a prerequisite for a candidate to satisfy the medical qualifications of being in accordance to SHAPE–I category to secure a grant of PC—'SHAPE' being an acronym where 'S' stands for psychological including cognitive function abnormalities, 'H' for hearing, 'A' for appendages, 'P' for physical capacity and 'E' for eyesight. It was submitted that while on the one hand, women officers sought parity with the male officers seeking the same status, a demand for a 'special and unjustified' treatment had been made out by them in their contention that they could not be held to the same standard of medical criteria as men.

Furthermore, as the yardstick to determine 'medical fitness' was a matter of policy, it was submitted that the court ought not to interfere with it. Therefore, the respondents argued that it was misconceived for the petitioners to contend that various mitigating factors and physiological changes that are specific to women were not accounted for at the evaluation.

b) *Second*, on the issue of the number of notified vacancies, the respondents submitted that it was conscious of the circumstances under which the SSB had been constituted to evaluate the petitioners. In the ordinary course, the number of vacancies per year for the grant of PC to officers was capped at 250. However, in order to implement the directions issued by the Supreme Court in *Babita Puniya* in letter and spirit, the said ceiling was relaxed by the respondents in the SSB constituted for women officers.

The respondents further countered the argument of the petitioners on setting the benchmark of assessing women officers at par with the score obtained by the last selected officer with lowest merit that particular year. The respondents claimed that it was a rational, reasonable and objective policy, which would enable the SSB to grant PC to officers on the basis of 'competitive merit'.

c) *Third*, inasmuch as the evaluation of the candidates on the basis of the ACRs was concerned, the respondents submitted that the SSB was conscious of the circumstances under which it had been constituted, and the underlying issues that would be faced by women officers owing to the manner in which their ACRs would have been filed by their former evaluators and superiors. Furthermore, since ACRs were merely one component of a larger evaluation exercise, there was no reason to apprehend the purported disadvantage that would weigh in at the time of their evaluation.

Supreme Court's Legal Analysis of Issues

The contentions advanced by both sides posed a fundamental question as to whether it was imperative for the respondents to evaluate women SSC officers on the same parameters as their male counterparts for awarding them an equivalent status in the armed forces. It appeared that even as the petitioners had overcome countless hurdles to reach the point that they had, as recognized in *Babita Puniya*, the criteria set out in the policy circular in respect of the grant of PC was structured in such a manner that the final hurdle had been made a little steeper—all in the guise of affording equal treatment for purportedly similarly situated persons.

While emphatically holding that the petitioners had been 'indirectly discriminated' by virtue of the subliminal barriers erected by respondents, the Supreme Court bench comprising Justices D.Y. Chandrachud and M.R. Shah favoured the adoption of a 'substantive approach' as opposed to a 'formal or symmetric approach' in the quest of achieving equality vis-à-vis the anti-discrimination guarantees enshrined by way of Articles 14 and 15(1) of the Constitution.[8]

The court traced the development and application of this distinction between formal and substantive equality, particularly in matters of employment and constitutional protections. Drawing from the learnings of other jurisdictions,[9] the court characterized 'indirect discrimination' as the outcome of the implementation of an instrument of law and recognized 'that actions taken on a seemingly innocent ground can in fact have discriminatory effects due to the structural inequalities that exist between classes'[10] and expounded on the how this 'neutrality' affects some more than the others. It reiterated the importance of the solemn duty cast upon the judiciary to be mindful of the various sections who have historically been subjected to discrimination, owing to numerous socio-economic disadvantages.

Therefore, to realize 'factual equality' as opposed to settling for the status quo of 'facial equality', it was acknowledged that courts would have to look closely at the ground realities, so as to ascertain the nature in which the discrimination alleged by a party unfolded[11] and to systematically weed out notions and practices that have seeped into institutions and structures, which unknowingly give an upper hand to the few at the cost of others.

Findings of the Court and Reliefs Granted to the Petitioners

Attributing the existence of indirect discrimination as not being conscious or malicious, but due to the inability to identify systemic biases and disadvantages, the court observed that 'the intention versus effects distinction is a sound jurisprudential basis on which to distinguish direct from indirect discrimination'.[12] It further held that requiring proof to establish discrimination would be an 'insuperable barrier' for a complainant and while affirming Fraser Test[13] reiterated that placing statistical evidence to demonstrate indirect discrimination before courts is only one of many ways in which a person seeking a remedy may establish their claims.

Most notably, however, the court opined that to conceptualize substantive equality, it was critical to employ an approach that combines tools to combat both direct and indirect discrimination, so as to holistically address the patterns and structures founded on such manifestations of discrimination. It underlined that the 'duty of constitutional courts, when confronted with such a scheme of things, would not just be to strike down the discriminatory practices and compensate for the harm hitherto arising out of them; but also structure adequate reliefs and remedies'.[14]

Applying its analysis to the facts of the case at hand, the Supreme Court ruled that the respondents' attempts at implementing a change in status quo, would inextricably involve a study of the systemic treatment, evaluation and impact of the prolonged denial of the rights sought by them. While at first blush, the respondents' attempts at implementing the directions in *Babita Puniya* were, as also alluded to by the Court of Justice of the European Union, seemingly 'neutral, innocent or good faith measures and policies adopted with no discriminatory intent whatsoever',[15] it observed that the application of such criteria most certainly resulted in the discriminatory treatment meted out to the petitioners at their respective evaluations. The court gave conclusive findings in respect of the specific issues argued by the parties:

a) *First*, the respondent's argument to justify their benchmark pertaining the petitioners qualifying for a grant PC by having to score higher than the lowest-scoring male candidate was found to be misplaced, even by their own admission, inasmuch as the ceiling limit of commissioning 250 officers per batch had not been breached in the past. Therefore, the object of evaluating women officers on the basis of inter se merit could not hold water, as there were multiple years when more than 250 male officers had been commissioned permanently. This revealed that the policy decision relied upon by the respondents had not been applied strictly. Moreover, in the respondent's own case, a one-time measure had been adopted so as to relax the ceiling limit of PC officers at 250 officers, considering the peculiar circumstances of the case made out by the petitioners, which in essence, left no merit in subjecting the petitioners through the process of having to attain the so-called objective benchmark to claim their right, which they were entitled to in the ordinary course.

b) *Second*, notwithstanding whether the respondents had any intent to discriminate against the petitioner while evaluating their claims inasmuch as the consideration of the ACRs were concerned, the court held that the systemic discrimination that women have faced in the army was reflected in the manner in which their performances and achievements had been taken into account. Women officers had never been recruited in the army with the object of being commissioned permanently, and their career growth was often stunted owing to limited progressive courses and options. This had led to the formation of a cyclical pattern of the discriminatory treatment meted out to them, hindering their evaluation that justified their prayers for 'special and unjustified treatment'. The court also observed that there was a need for a comprehensive review of the method of evaluation of ACRs of women officers, keeping in mind the systemic discrimination faced by them, which was evidenced by the disproportionate impact on their career progression.

c) *Third*, noting that while the aspect of medical requirements was consistently applied, and that the metric adopted by the respondents in the form of 'SHAPE – I' level fitness is not per se arbitrary, the court held that it was certainly disadvantageous for the petitioners to be subjected to a rigorous scrutiny of their fitness levels at a belated stage in their respective careers. Such a requirement being imposed upon women officers in their middle age as opposed to men, who are evaluated for the same position in their prime physical condition, was unfair and contrary to the guarantees under Articles 14 and 15(1) of the Constitution.

After analysing the material placed before it for consideration and examining the merits of the arguments advanced, the Supreme Court concluded that the pattern of evaluation devised for the implementation of the directions issued by it in *Babita Puniya* was discriminatory in nature.[16] It observed that women officers had faced a blow-back of systemic discrimination that was evident in the neutral criteria of evaluation set out by the respondents, that had 'prevented them from enjoying the full panoply of entitlements'.[17]

Impact of the Judgment in Nitisha's Case, and a Reality Check

Jurisprudentially speaking, this decision of the Supreme Court has since been hailed as a stepping stone to tackle indirect discrimination of citizens and minimizing arbitrariness, as it has provided courts with plausible solutions to identify such situations and implement measures to remedy the situation in the present, as well as to avoid repetitive patterns for the future. While cases involving indirect discrimination will require a thorough analysis specific to the facts of each case, the precedential value of this decision will be put to test when similar situations are brought to the fore. A commitment to ensuring substantive equality, requires not only the quashing of a discriminatory practice and immediate remedial measures to undo the effects thereof, but also to predict the outcomes of patterns of systemic discrimination in institutions. This is aptly explained by the Canadian Supreme Court stating that the guarantee against discrimination was 'not to punish the discriminator, but rather to provide relief for the victims of discrimination'.[18] This decision was rendered in the context of a corporation dispensing with the services of an employee, who, as a part of her religious practice, was forbidden from working from sundown on Friday to sundown on Saturday.

While such directory diktats of courts to the Union government and the army seem promising and indicate a change in the tide, there is yet a lot to be done. Even after the Supreme Court's decision in *Nitisha*, there are various issues in the implementation of the said directions. While women officers had been granted PC along with all other consequential promotions and benefits, the realization of the latter has proven to be a fresh challenge. Women officers allege that they have been made to compete for promotions against junior officers who have joined subsequently instead of being evaluated against male counterparts from their corresponding batches, who were promoted long ago. The redressal of such grievance also found favour with the Supreme Court when, on 3 November 2023, it disposed an application[19] moved in *Nitisha*. Until a level playing field is provided for women officers, it is only a matter of time that the courts will be flooded with similar such petitions, rendering this extensive and detailed doctrinal analysis of the Supreme Court nugatory.

Another aspect that has arisen pursuant to the gaps in the implementation of the directions in *Nitisha*, is that while women officers have secured promotions to the rank of (full) colonels, being denied the right to hold command positions, they are yet to receive their due recognition. This issue has been judicially noticed by the Supreme Court, which has observed that even if such promotions are given, women officers are more often than not offered such postings that they are left with no option but to opt for a lesser entitlement. This is in addition to other administrative issues pertaining to release of the financial benefits.

Notwithstanding the progress made thus far, the battle is far from over, and constitutional courts are bound to be called upon by various stakeholders to evaluate and strike a balance between the claims of the disadvantaged vis-à-vis the requirements of the institution. It is, therefore, imperative that all stakeholders are vigilant and diligent at identifying discrimination in any form and take steps to weed out the same while simultaneously suggesting remedial measures. This will only happen when one acknowledges that women officers 'are not adjuncts to a male-dominated establishment whose presence must be "tolerated" within narrow confines',[20] and that their service is as essential as anyone tasked with defending our great nation.

Pregnancy Discrimination in the Workplace—the Chasm between Law and Practice

Francisca Pretorius

Monu Kumari v. Staff Selection Commission

Between the idea
and the reality
between the motion
and the act
falls the Shadow

—T.S. Eliot, 'The Hollow Men'

For as long as women have been able to participate in the workforce, they have encountered gender discrimination. Even in the twenty-first century, when women's rights have been enshrined in legislation, the spectre of unequal treatment looms large as they navigate professional spheres.

Women in the workforce face a myriad of challenges, including lack of access to employment opportunities, unequal pay, harassment, stereotyping and barriers to promotion. Notably, women working in predominantly male environments report experiencing significantly higher rates of discrimination.[1]

One particularly insidious type of discrimination women face is around the fundamental right to choose parenthood. Pregnancy discrimination, often rooted in the misperception of pregnancy as a disability or an undue burden to employers, not only undermines a woman's autonomy but also perpetuates archaic stereotypes. These stereotypes wrongfully suggest that motherhood diminishes a woman's commitment and capabilities in the workplace. Contrary to this outdated perception, working mothers frequently demonstrate increased efficiency[2] and empathy,[3] which are invaluable to any team. Moreover, organizations with female executives in leadership roles tend to outperform their counterparts.[4]

I vividly recall my first job interview fresh out of law school, where I was brazenly asked about my plans for pregnancy in the near future. Such discriminatory queries frequently catch women off guard and, because of unequal power dynamics, often leave them to either respond uncomfortably (like I did) or endure silently, allowing the injustice to prevail unchallenged. While the fundamental right to non-discrimination is guaranteed in many modern constitutions, sadly, the promise of equality enshrined in law too often remains unrealized in practice.

The past few decades have seen many nations enact legislations intended to end gender discrimination in the workplace. Yet, the gap between legal mandates and actual implementation remains stubbornly wide. It is within this landscape that the case of *Monu Kumari* emerges as a glimmer of hope. This case delves into the fundamental rights of pregnant women in India, shining a light on the ongoing struggle for gender equality in the workforce. Through its examination, we glimpse not only the persistent challenges women face, but also the potential for judicial intervention to close the chasm between legislation and practice and rectify systemic injustices.

The Facts of the Case

The case of *Monu Kumari v. Staff Selection Commission & Ors*,[5] heard and decided by the High Court of Delhi before Justices Vipin Sanghi and Rekha Palli, addressed the rights of pregnant women in matters of public employment.

The petitioner, Monu Kumari, was a constable serving in the Delhi Police when she saw an advertisement issued for the recruitment of sub-inspectors in Delhi Police and Central Armed Police Forces. Pursuant to the advertisement, Kumari applied for the position and appeared for the first written examination of the recruitment process. Based on her good performance in the initial examination, Kumari provisionally qualified for the eligibility test, physical endurance test (PET, for short) and a medical examination.

In May 2013, Kumari discovered that she was pregnant and upon learning this news, she requested accommodation from the Staff Selection Commission (SSC) to postpone her PET and medical examination scheduled for October 2013. Despite her pregnancy, the SSC denied her request, citing a clause in the advertisement stipulating '. . . the candidature of female candidates who are pregnant at the time of Physical Endurance Test will be rejected as they cannot undergo PET. No appeal/representation will be entertained against such rejection.' The SSC requested that she proceed with the test. For understandable and commonsensical reasons, she decided not to attend her PET.

Feeling aggrieved by the lack of accommodation by the SSC, Kumari filed a petition (known as Original Application) before the Central Administrative Tribunal, challenging the impugned stipulation in the recruitment advertisement and seeking relief that the SSC recognize her candidature as valid for the selection and process her application accordingly.

The Tribunal, however, dismissed Kumari's application, upholding the validity of the advertisement. It held that since the recruitment advertisement clearly stipulated the condition regarding pregnant candidates and the rejection of their candidature, Kumari was bound by it. Dissatisfied with the Tribunal's decision, Kumari filed a writ petition before the Delhi High Court to challenge the rejection of her application and the validity of the offending clause in the advertisement.

In the Delhi High Court, Kumari's primary argument was that the advertisement discriminated against pregnant women, treating pregnancy as a disability or misfortune. She contended that this discrimination violated women's fundamental rights enshrined in the Constitution of India, as well as the Maternity Benefit Act, 1961—a law that protects the employment of and provides benefits to women for a certain period before and after childbirth. Kumari asserted that debarring her from consideration for employment due to her pregnancy, a natural phenomenon, violated her right to life and personal liberty.

The high court agreed with Kumari, finding the condition outlined in the advertisement unconstitutional. By now, Kumari had given birth to her child, and the court ordered the respondents to proceed with conducting the PET and medical examinations for her. The court further held that if Kumari proved to be successful and she secured more marks than the last selected candidate in the recruitment category, she must be appointed to the post and be granted seniority and pay fixation on a notional basis from the date other candidates selected in the same process were granted. She was however not entitled to arrears of pay for the period she had not physically worked, as per directions of the court. Furthermore, the high court instructed the SSC to ensure that no such discriminatory clause is included in any of their future advertisements. The attitude of the SSC in treating Monu Kumari at a disadvantage because of her pregnancy was sharply taken note of by the court in the following terms:

Good fortune smiled upon the petitioner, when, in the second half of the month of May, 2013, she learnt that she was pregnant. Thus, she carried in her womb, the promise for future generations of our species. This fortune of the petitioner, unfortunately, has been turned into her misfortune by the respondents, who seem to view pregnancy as a calamity; disease, or; disability.

Enshrined Rights

The discussion on basic human rights enshrined in the Constitution of India in this case is paramount. The Delhi High Court provided a clear and detailed legal foundation for finding the advertisement unconstitutional by focusing its analysis on Part III of the Fundamental Rights of the Constitution of India, specifically Articles 14, 16 and 21.

Article 14 of the Constitution enshrines the principle of equality before the law, and read with Article 15, this is a fundamental right available to all Indian citizens, regardless of their religion, race, caste, sex or place of birth. Article 14 mandates that the State shall not deny to any person equality before the law or equal protection of the laws within the territory of India. In the context of this case, the recruitment advertisement effectively rejected pregnant women's eligibility for public employment based solely on their pregnancy status, treating certain women different than other candidates. Notably, the advertisement did not prohibit women from applying for the positions in question, nor did it state that being pregnant disqualifies a woman for appointment.

Article 16 guarantees equality of opportunity in matters of public employment and prohibits discrimination on grounds of religion, race, caste, sex, descent, place of birth or residence. The objective of Article 16 is to ensure that all citizens have an equal opportunity to compete for public employment without facing discrimination based on irrelevant factors. In *Kumari*'s case, the advertisement for recruitment excluded pregnant women from fully participating in the recruitment process, and the SSC explicitly denied her request for a delay in her PET and medical examinations.

Most importantly, Article 21 of the Constitution protects the right to life and personal liberty. The Delhi High Court emphatically held in its ruling that choosing motherhood is 'at the epicentre of [women's] right to life and personal liberty'. Choosing to become a parent, getting pregnant and pregnancy are natural aspects of a woman's life, and denying employment opportunities to women based on their pregnancy status infringes upon their right to life and personal liberty. By upholding the recruitment advertisement, the tribunal effectively deprived Kumari of her right to pursue her chosen career path and earn a livelihood for herself and her family.

Discussing the interplay of the rights guaranteed by the Constitution of India, the Delhi High Court succinctly, in the concluding part of the judgment, observed as under:

In a society such as ours where women struggle everyday against the confines of patriarchy to seek parity with their male counterparts in all walks of life, including the professional sphere, ousting pregnant women altogether from the selection process for public employment amounts to discriminating against women in matters of public employment for reasons solely attributable to their sex. This is not only in violation of the constitutional mandate as embodied in Article 14, which guarantees equality as a fundamental right available to all citizens of India, irrespective of their religion, race, caste, sex or place of birth, but is also against the very fibre of Article 16, which ensures equality of opportunity to all in matters of public employment. Furthermore, the aforesaid condition essentially disadvantages women for making choices such as motherhood, that are at the epicentre of their right to life and personal liberty. It needs no gainsaying that motherhood cannot be an excuse to exclude women from public employment— whether directly or indirectly and, it is for this reason that we are of the view that the condition stipulated in Note II is violative of Articles 14, 16 and 21 of the Constitution of India.

During the proceedings, Kumari's counsel relied heavily on the decision of the Rajasthan High Court in *Laxmi Devi v. State of Rajasthan*,[6] a case that dealt with a similar issue, and the Delhi High Court quoted this case extensively in its judgment as well. The Rajasthan High Court had held that denying maternity benefits to pregnant women in public employment was arbitrary and violated their constitutional rights. The court had emphasized that pregnancy is a natural consequence of marriage and any distinction made on its ground would be considered arbitrary and violative of Article 14 of the Constitution.

The Incontrovertible Chasm between Law and Practice

In light of the constitutional provisions and legal principles comprehensively discussed by the Delhi High Court, the ruling appears unequivocal—that by denying Kumari's accommodation request for a delayed PET and medical examination, the SSC clearly discriminated against her on the basis of pregnancy, thus infringing upon her rights guaranteed under the Constitution of India. The analysis and conclusion seem as straightforward as a basic question in a first-year constitutional law class. Yet, despite this apparent clarity, justice for Mona Kumari remained elusive for six years. This raises the critical question: *why does the guarantee of equality under the law often fails to translate into practice?*

Glimmer of Hope: Systemic Change

The Delhi High Court's ruling in *Kumari's* case was notable for its broader implications beyond the specific circumstances of the petitioner. Rather than confining its decision to the specific case at hand, the court took a proactive stance by prohibiting the inclusion of discriminatory clauses in future advertisements, signifying a shift towards addressing systemic issues and not just offering individual remedies. This precedent puts public employers (and potentially private organizations) on notice to re-evaluate and amend their recruitment policies to ensure compliance with constitutional and legal protections against discrimination. While it remains to be seen how this judicial imperative will manifest in practical terms, the ruling marks a significant step towards not only embedding equality in legal frameworks but also actively enforcing it in practice.

Justice Delayed Is Justice (Almost) Denied

An issue not directly addressed in the matter but one that caught my attention is the fact that *Monu Kumari*'s case was initiated in 2013, and then the legal battle endured for six years before finally being decided in 2019. This brings to mind the adage 'justice delayed is justice denied'. Had Monu Kumari not persisted in pursuing her case, justice might have remained elusive, and there would have been no systemic change. Of course, this delay is not specifically gendered, but how many women choose to not even try because they do not have the energy to fight for this long, without any guarantee of success? A delay such as this one deters other women from seeking recourse through the legal system, highlighting the intimidating nature of protracted legal proceedings. Though, of course, in this particular case the Delhi High Court very pertinently and sensitively protected her seniority and minimized her loss.

Furthermore, the protracted legal process underscores broader issues of judicial backlog and inefficiency. Beyond the specifics of *Monu Kumari*'s case, such delays erode trust in the judiciary and inflict tangible harm on individuals awaiting resolution. For Monu Kumari, the years of waiting not only exemplified the arduousness of legal proceedings but also underscored the systemic inequities inherent within the system.

Comparative Example: South Africa

When South Africa, my home country, transitioned to a democracy in 1994, it embraced one of the most progressive constitutions in the world. The Constitution's Bill of Rights specifically identifies pregnancy as a basis for unfair discrimination.[7] Additionally, various labour acts, including the 'Employment Equity Act',[8] the 'Labour Relations Act',[9] and the 'Code of Good Practice on the Protection of Employees During Pregnancy and After the Birth of a Child',[10] offer further safeguards for pregnant employees. Despite these robust legal protections, their application in practice, particularly in the armed forces, often falls short. A stark illustration of this is a case where a base commander was brought before the Equality Court for demeaning pregnant women in front of their peers and threatening them with immediate transfers due to their pregnancy.[11]

Comparative Example: USA

. . . we commence with the premise that one does not have a constitutional right to remain in the armed services. But the Marine Corps, instead of taking an individualized approach to the disability of pregnancy, established a general rule that seriously affects the ability of women Marines who are physically able to be mobile and ready and for personal or religious reasons care to give birth and give a child away for adoption or to a willing family or husband for on-duty care. Like the pregnancy leave regulations in [Cleveland Board of Education v] LaFleur,[12] the mandatory discharge regulation is overbroad and overly restrictive because it penalizes the decision to bear a child by those Marines whose mobility and readiness would not be reduced, either during most months preceding birth or during their careers after birth. The Marine Corps general rule may also be counterproductive because the penalty of discharge can lead women to ignore or conceal pregnancy as long as possible to avoid diagnosis and discharge.[13]

The United States is another country where the legal rights are (mostly) enshrined but remain unrealized in practice. Initially, during the 1950s, regulations mandated the discharge of women serving in the armed forces if they became pregnant.[14] This policy changed following the 1976 *Crawford v. Cushman* case[15] quoted above, which deemed the regulation unconstitutional as it violated the Fifth Amendment's guarantees of due process and equal protection under the United States Constitution. Despite the landmark *Crawford* case, the Pregnancy Discrimination Act of 1978,[16] which prohibits employment discrimination based on pregnancy, childbirth or related medical conditions, does not extend its protection to the military. Even though there have been policy updates in recent years to classify pregnancy discrimination as a form of illegal sex discrimination, women in the armed forces, almost five decades post-*Crawford*, continue to encounter adverse career consequences due to pregnancy.[17]

Conclusion: A Cultural Shift

Revisiting the crucial question: why does the legal promise of equality often falter in real-world scenarios, whether in India or globally? I believe the heart of the issue lies in the prevalent implicit biases against pregnant women, who are unfairly labelled as burdensome and perceived as less capable or even disabled. To effectively challenge and dismantle these entrenched perceptions, a deliberate cultural transformation is essential.

While legal frameworks and court decisions, such as the *Monu Kumari* case, mark significant progress towards recognizing and safeguarding pregnant women's rights, they alone cannot bridge the chasm between law and lived reality. The principles upheld in these judgments need to be integrated into workplace cultures across diverse sectors and regions, fostering an environment where women are not forced to choose between their careers and motherhood. Achieving such a profound cultural (r)evolution is vital to nurturing a genuinely inclusive and fair professional realm for all women, where their rights are not merely inscribed in legal texts but are fully experienced in their everyday lives.

5

Can Women Be Ambitious and Pregnant?

Professor Shruti Bedi

Neetu Bala v. Union of India

You can have ambition, but not too much
You should aim to be successful, but not too successful
Otherwise, you will threaten the man.

This excerpt from Chimamanda Ngozi Adichie's TEDx speech[1] unequivocally addresses the deeply engrained patriarchal social construct that deems it unacceptable for women not only to work, but more significantly, to achieve success. Beyoncé, the well-known singer, features this part of Adichie's speech in her song 'Flawless'.[2] The missive being that women are expected to don *smaller* roles so as not to threaten the space that is dominated by men. They are taught to step back and shrink their opportunities and their space.

As women enter workplaces and professions that are traditionally male-dominated, there is an increasing need to understand and counter hidden gender biases. It is important to also recognize that simple eradication of formal discrimination is insufficient to address circumstances such as childbearing and the resulting concerns of working women.

The Factual Canvas

The High Court of Punjab and Haryana had the occasion to deal with the issue of hidden bias against women in 2016 in the case of *Neetu Bala v. Union of India* presided over by Justice Harinder Singh Sidhu.[3] The matter concerned challenging the denial of employment by the Army Medical Corps (AMC) to a woman solely on account of her pregnancy. The issue arose when the Ministry of Defence issued an advertisement inviting either male or female applicants for grant of Short Service Commission (SSC) in the AMC. The eligibility conditions required the applicant to have passed the final year MBBS examination and be under the age of forty years as on 31 December 2013. There was no condition stipulating that the candidate had to be unmarried. The petitioner, who fulfilled the eligibility conditions being an MBBS, MD was successful in the interview held on 10 June 2013 and was intimated that she was selected for grant of SSC in the rank of captain. Although she was initially declared unfit in the medical examination on 11 June 2013, she was subsequently declared medically fit by the Appeal Medical Board on 16 July 2013 and was issued an appointment letter dated 16 January 2014. The appointment letter stated that she had been found fit by the medical board, but she would be required to undergo medical inspection on reporting to the unit to simply confirm that there was no deterioration in her health status.

As desired, she reported for duty on 10 February 2014 to the commandant of Military Hospital, Pathankot for commencement of employment. After her medical examination, she was informed that she was medically fit and free from contagious disease. However, they noted that she was seven months pregnant but with no complications, and since there were no clear guidelines on whether pregnancy could be construed as 'deterioration of health', she was asked to wait pending clarification on the matter from the headquarters. Thereafter, on 20 February 2014, she was informed that she was unfit to join service. This decision was based on the terms and conditions of service of officers granted SSC (Army Instructions 75/78), wherein the letter dated 22 October 2009 provided that all female candidates would be screened for pregnancy and detection of the same would render a candidate 'unfit' for commissioning.

Upon receiving the communication of denial of appointment, the petitioner requested that the vacancy be kept for her so that she could join service after delivering the child. Receiving no response on her request, she petitioned the Punjab and Haryana High Court. The Union of India contended that since the petitioner was seven months pregnant, she was not in a position to undertake the strenuous physical training activities or service in the field that was expected from a newly commissioned medical officer. Further, justifying the denial of request to keep the post vacant till delivery, it was stated that that as per the offer of appointment, no request of change of service, place of posting or extension of date of joining could be accepted. The vacancy which had remained unsubscribed due to any reason was to be passed on to the next candidate in the merit list prepared at the time of interview.

The question before the high court, therefore, was whether 'the denial of appointment to the petitioner holding her to be "unfit" solely on account of pregnancy is legal and justified?'

The court upheld the claim of the petitioner that pregnancy could not be treated as a disqualification for appointment in the AMC. The reasoning of the court was based on both national and international jurisprudence on the subject and merits close attention.

Is Pregnancy a Disqualification?

The court held that denial of appointment to the petitioner on the pretext of pregnancy was against the mandate of Articles 14, 15 and 16. Article 16 specifically prohibited gender discrimination (pregnancy disability) in matters of public employment. Citing precedents from India and the US, Justice Harinder Singh Sidhu, in para 24 observed:

> . . . in cases where a married woman is not disqualified
> for appointment, the fact that she is pregnant, cannot
> be a disqualification for continuing with appointment.
> Nor can pregnancy, in such circumstances, be treated as
> a bar to be appointed. Any inability to discharge duties
> during the months, before and after childbirth, can be
> taken care of by granting maternity leave for the period
> required.[4]

The Constitution of India provides the basis for challenging such exclusionary and facially innocent practices circumscribing women's employment opportunities based on pregnancy. The act of exclusion of women from employment based on pregnancy confirms the second-class standing of women in workplaces. The decision of the court in prohibiting pregnancy discrimination is significant, as it strikes at the societal assumption that rationalizes inequality and discrimination with seemingly neutral rules that justify gendered discrimination.

Organizational structures often carry cultural and gender biases. Pregnant women in particular are perceived as burdensome because they may not align with the idealized 'male worker norm'. Men, on the other hand, are commonly assumed to exhibit higher commitment levels, unencumbered by the responsibilities of bearing and rearing children. These perceptions contribute to the perpetuation of a patriarchal perspective, suggesting that women cannot effectively balance the roles of being good mothers and competent workers simultaneously.

Rules that deny employment to women based on the temporary condition of being pregnant are discriminatory and arbitrary. The court, by holding that where a married women is not otherwise disqualified for appointment, her being pregnant cannot be a disqualification, controverted the established societal perception against a pregnant woman. Pregnancy is not a disability but is a natural consequence of marriage and married life.[5] Such exclusionary practices against women are incorrectly and stereotypically justified on the basis of women's reproductive role. The assumption that pregnancy is incompatible with certain jobs is the severest in fields where women have historically faced isolation.

The Punjab and Haryana High Court further held in *Neetu Bala* that such treatment of pregnant women would 'fall foul of Article 42 of the Constitution which requires the State to make provision for securing just and humane conditions of work and for maternity relief' (para 25). It may be pointed out that Article 42 is a Directive Principle of State Policy and, as a result, is not directly enforceable. Nevertheless, it is available for determining the legal validity of the discriminatory action. Directive Principles cannot be disregarded entirely, effort must be employed to provide a relevant role for them in constitutional interpretation. They must be used to concretize the abstract concepts of fundamental rights. In simple terms, they must be used to enhance the meaning of fundamental freedoms and rights.

Discrimination and Equality Jurisprudence

Interestingly, the court also referred to international conventions in addition to constitutional principles. Para 26 propagated the view that such 'conventions would be enforceable when they elucidate and effectuate the fundamental rights and that the courts are obliged to apply them when there is no inconsistency with the domestic law'. It particularly relied on two such conventions—the Convention on the Elimination of all Forms of Discrimination against Women (CEDAW), 1979; and International Labour Organization (ILO): Maternity Protection Convention, 2000. Both the conventions reiterate that discrimination against women violate the principles of equality of rights and respect for human dignity. In the process, the court stressed the need for 'substantive equality' as opposed to merely 'formal equality'. Substantive equality focuses not on sameness or difference, but on group-based disadvantage. Formal equality treats two groups that are similar, identically; while substantive equality raises the question as to whether a rule or practice perpetuates group-based disadvantage, in which case it falls foul of the equality guarantee. Guided by such notions of equality, the court in para 34 held that the international conventions required 'State/parties to take all appropriate measures to eliminate discrimination against women in the field of employment and provide the same employment opportunities, including the application of the same criteria for selection in matters of employment.'

Most organizations are readily inclined to exclude a pregnant employee from their workforce, especially when it is in their economic self-interest, or even when it is not. Eliminating pregnancy discrimination requires confronting this mindset of antipathy towards a pregnant employee. It is time to treat pregnancy simply as a normal state of any individual without perceiving it as a means to perpetuate inequality. The court further took recourse to decisions of the English courts and the European Court of Justice to observe in para 58 that:

> As only women can become pregnant and as such only women can be refused employment on the ground of pregnancy, hence a refusal for employment on the ground of pregnancy constitutes *direct discrimination on the ground of sex*, even though the refusal may be occasioned by adverse financial consequences to the employer for finding a replacement for the duration of the pregnancy.[6]

It is true that workforce differentials between men and women continue to exist. Employers exhibit reluctance to employ women especially where the risk of career interruption would be detrimental to the functioning of the organization, and where the cost of such interruption is relatively high. Refusal of employment on the ground of pregnancy amounts to direct gender discrimination. Article 16 of the Indian Constitution strikes at the very root of such discrimination. Reproductive difference cannot become the basis of denial of equality towards a particular gender. Such differential practices serve to ensure women's secondary socio-economic status. Exclusionary treatment of pregnant women in workplaces cannot be justified on the basis of employer difficulty.

Para 67 of the judgment importantly held, 'Most of all by forcing a choice between bearing a child and employment, it interferes both, with her reproductive rights and her right to employment. Such an action can have no place in modern India.'[7]

Justice Sidhu's observation that it is unacceptable to push a woman to make a choice between bearing a child and employment, is remarkable as it urges us to understand the consequence of such action. We need policies that embrace accommodation of pregnancy within the work culture. Denial of such accommodation amounts to denial of both her reproductive rights as well as her right to employment. The Constitution provides for social equality for women, and rejection of employment creates a disability for working women that will have lasting effects not only on their ability to earn but also on their standing in society.

A similar stance was adopted by the Supreme Court of India in its recent judgment delivered on 14 February 2024 in *Union of India v. Ex Lt Selina John*.[8] The Division Bench of Justices Sanjiv Khanna and Dipankar Datta held that the rule that mandated the discharge of women nursing officers from service on the ground that they got married was arbitrary on the face of it and that it amounted to 'a coarse case of gender discrimination and inequality'. The court opined that such patriarchal rules undermined 'human dignity, right to non-discrimination and fair treatment'. Taking a stringent view of such attitude, the court ordered a payment of Rs 60 lakh (6 million) as compensation to the officer. It is true that rules resulting in the disentitlement of women employees on account of any type of domestic involvement cannot be held valid under the Constitution.

Conclusion

Eliminating discrimination related to pregnancy will require a concerted effort to dismantle the historical prejudices against a woman's right to earn a living and being economically independent. The solution does not lie in denying the difference, but in restructuring the institutions that have constructed its social meaning. The attempt to establish meaningful equality between working men and women must commence with the willingness amongst employers to formulate rules and regulations that encourage women to overcome the barrier of expected fertility. This end would be served by re-examining the national policies governing workplaces.

The Constitution of India does not simply guarantee formal equality but strikes at the entrenched power structures that have attained the status of 'normalcy' after decades of being treated as immutable. It is time to rectify the tradition of treating pregnancy as a disability and consequently as a valid differential at workplaces. The Indian Constitution recognizes gender equality which must be furthered to dissect the established inegalitarian societal norms. That is the profound vision of our transformative Constitution.

The Punjab and Haryana High Court in the landmark judgment in *Neetu Bala v. Union of India*, successfully questioned the seemingly innocuous penalization of pregnancy amongst working women and made a significant contribution towards our Constitution's anti-discrimination jurisprudence and its commitment to social justice. It recognized that pregnancy is not an obstacle to a woman who is desirous of earning her living and making her mark in hitherto male-dominated vocations. This case illustrates the power of legal intervention in shaping constitutional principles of gender jurisprudence, urging a more comprehensive perspective as society moves towards an inclusive understanding of justice.

6

Pregnant or Unwilling?

Aishwarya Bhati and Chitrangda Rastravara

Inspector (Mahila) Ravina v. Union of India

*What peculiarly defines the situation of a woman is that she is a free and autonomous being like all human creatures—nevertheless finds herself living in a world where men compel her to assume the status of the 'Other'. They propose to turn her into an object of doom to immanence since her transcendence is to be overshadowed and forever transcended by another consciousness which is itself essential and sovereign. The drama of woman lies in this conflict between the fundamental aspirations of every subject—who always regards the self as the essential and the compulsions of a situation in which she is the inessential—*Simone de Beauvoir

In the 1970s and 1980s, feminist writers and philosophers began exploring the relationship between motherhood and pregnancy and their interplay with labour and the workforce, as well as the social and cultural implicational aspects of views on these topics. Many notable writers such as Simone de Beauvoir, Adrienne Rich and Helen Deutsch wrote on how society viewed women during pregnancy and childbirth and as new mothers.[1] One of the most influential works on this subject is by the philosopher and writer Adrienne Rich, who distinguishes two meanings of motherhood as 'one which is superimposed on the other; the potential relationship of any woman to her powers of reproduction and children; and the institution, which aims to ensure that all women shall remain under male control'.[2] She describes this as the keystone of social and political systems which withholds one half of the human species from crucial and essential decisions that affect the course of their lives.

We are all 'born of woman' said Adrienne Rich, categorizing it as a 'universal truth'. Anyone who has observed any young mother, whether a tiny bird, fish, insect, reptile, mighty elephant or any other form in the animal kingdom, either in nature or television, would immediately relate. A bare observation of the behaviour, actions and skills of new mothers, across the blue planet, irrespective of species, reveals a pattern of extraordinary grit, determination, dedication and strength that far exceeds the yardstick. It makes for legendary stories too! The human world has always treated its young mothers with the greatest of respect, dignity, protection and affection. However, the modern world has been in a state of churn on how to treat young mothers, who have chosen to participate in the workforce rather than just be content with playing the *traditional, culturally accepted* roles of mother and nurturer. The journey has been arduous and painful. Starting from treating motherhood as a disqualification, taboo, incapacity and incompetence, we have progressed to recognition of the right of reproductive choice, amongst some international covenants and constitutional guarantees of many modern and progressive democracies.

India is strongly a pro-choice democracy, which manifestly and firmly recognizes the right of equal opportunity for all and takes it a step further by employing the Doctrine of Affirmative Action in favour of women, children and other marginalized sections of society, to realize and achieve substantive equality in true sense. Reproductive choice and decisional autonomy of a woman is recognized as a fundamental right under the Indian Constitution. Recognition as a fundamental right allows the constitutional courts of India to exercise the power of judicial review over legislative and executive action, to examine whether there is any unfair, arbitrary or unreasonable infringement of reproductive choice and decisional autonomy of a woman, and to strike it down in case of any violation thereof.

A discussion on indirect discrimination towards women who are pregnant or are young mothers is incomplete without a debate on the question of 'equality'. A straightforward view here is not useful as general feminist theory revolves around the concept of 'formal equality' where the comparator or yardstick is the 'male norm' against which the treatment of women is to be understood.[3] This approach would require women to conform to these norms in order to be considered equal, which is simply not possible for understanding equality and equal treatment before law in respect of women who are pregnant or young mothers. This is the question addressed by the Delhi High Court in 2015, adjudicated upon by Justices S. Ravindra Bhat and V.K. Shali in the case of *Inspector (Mahila) Ravina v. Union of India & Ors*,[4] where the high court recognized and upheld the manner in which certain norms would inherently only affect women more than men.

The Facts of the Case

This case before the Delhi High Court highlighted an extraordinary factual matrix where a young woman inspector of the Central Reserve Police Force (CRPF), aggrieved by the action of the official respondents in promoting her to the post of assistant commandant belatedly, in comparison to her batchmates, chose to invoke the jurisdiction of the Delhi High Court. The reason stated by the respondents for this delayed promotion of the petitioner was her inability to participate in a pre-promotional course, along with her batchmates, known as the 'Mandatory Field Service Criteria'. The criterion required the petitioner to serve two years in a duty battalion or an operational post which she could not on account of her pregnancy. She subsequently cleared the promotional course in the next batch. However, her seniority was forfeited by applying a Standing Order (in the nature of a General Executive Order), which prescribed that in situations where candidates show unwillingness to perform the course on compassionate grounds, their chance would be preserved, but seniority shall be forfeited.

It is notable to also direct attention to three key facts of the case that summarize how the situation described by feminist writers years ago remains true for the world we live in today. First, the official reasons ascribed for the forfeiture of seniority of the petitioner was that she had shown unwillingness to attend the promotional course to maintain her seniority. Second, the respondents also conceded that the petitioner was denied an opportunity to participate in the said pre-promotional course on the ground of her pregnancy. Lastly and ironically, her batchmates who were unable to attend the said course were not only allowed to attend the next courses but were also granted seniority since the establishment recognized that their deployment was involuntary and due to circumstances outside of their control.

Does Absence Due to Pregnancy Really Amount to 'Unwillingness to Attend'?

The main question for determination before the Delhi High Court was whether the petitioner's pregnancy would amount to unwillingness to attend a required promotional course and whether she was entitled to a relaxation of rules to claim seniority at par with her batchmates. Curiously, in this case, the petitioner had not even expressly pleaded pregnancy-based discrimination or indirect discrimination. However, despite this technical flaw, the Delhi High Court examined this question and found it to be a classic case of pregnancy-based discrimination or indirect discrimination.

The Delhi High Court categorically held that pregnancy *did not* amount to unwillingness to participate and noted that consequential denial of seniority based on such a reasoning by the respondent would contravene the mandate of Articles 14, 21 as well as 42 alongside the provisions of the Maternity Benefits Act, 1976, the Factories Act, 1948 and the Central Civil Service (Leave) Rules, 1972. The high court categorically held in its decision that:

> To conclude that pregnancy amounts to mere unwillingness as the respondents did in this case was indefensible. The choice to bear a child is not only a deeply personal one for a family but is also a physically taxing time for the mother. This right to reproduction and child rearing is an essential facet of Article 21 of the Constitution; it is underscored by the commitment of the Constitution framers to ensure that circumstances conducive to the exercise of this choice are created and maintained by the State at all times. This commitment is signified by Article 42 ("Provision for just and humane conditions of work and maternity relief—The State shall provide conditions for securing just and humane conditions of work and for maternity relief") and Article 45 ("Provision for early childhood care and

education to children below the age of six years—The State shall endeavour to provide for early childhood care . . ."). The Maternity Benefits Act, 1976 protects the expecting mother's interests in employment. Provisions of the Factories Act, 1948 and the Central Civil Service (Leave) Rules, 1972 provide for postnatal care leave enabling mothers to spend time with infants who need early childhood care.[5]

Indirect discrimination or pregnancy-based discrimination stems from gender stereotypes of the employer which often leave women vulnerable both in terms of pay as well as continued employment. Sociologists often remark that such institutional biases view pregnant women as employees who may not be 'ideal', that is, someone 'resolutely committed, flexible and singularly focussed on their job'.[6] A pregnant woman often does not conform to this unrealistic expectation of the 'ideal' set by the organizations that employ them. In addition to denial of opportunity, many pregnant women face biases when it comes to job assignments as well as rewards, as is evident in the present case. In this case, the CRPF's position, as rightly observed by the Delhi High Court, was that they deemed 'Pregnancy is a departure from an employee's "normal" condition and to equate both sets of public employees, i.e. those who do not have to make such choice and those who do (like the petitioner) and apply the same standards mechanically is discriminatory'.[7] It is rather unfortunate that when it comes to the treatment of pregnant women across several nations, a common thread appears; similar patterns of discrimination against pregnant women are noticed that highlight the pervasive nature of indirect discrimination in workspaces in relation to pay, promotion, rewards and in some cases, even continuance of employment. Deeply aware of such biases, many working women across the world find themselves choosing between a successful professional career or fulfilling the desire to bear children at some stage in their lives. A choice that seems not only impossible and irrational but also rooted in unequal treatment of women in comparison to male employees who may not face such a conundrum. It also trespasses on the autonomy a woman may have over her body, including whether or not she would like to bear children as it directly affects her ability and choice to do so. The Delhi High Court unequivocally recognized that the treatment of the petitioner by the respondents in the present case was clearly discriminatory and also observed that it would be a travesty of justice if a female public employee is forced to choose between having a child and her career.

Further, the Delhi High Court also noted that in circumstances like this, unlike 'plain unwillingness' on the part of an officer to undertake the course, which may possibly lead to loss of seniority, the choice to bear children or become a parent as exercised by a female employee stands on an entirely different footing. In view of this rationale, the Delhi High Court categorically held:

If the latter is treated as expressing unwillingness, CRPF would clearly violate Article 21. As between a male official and female official, there is no distinction, in regard to promotional avenues, none was asserted. In fact, there is a common pre-promotional programme which both have to undergo; both belong to a common cadre. In these circumstances, the denial of seniority benefit to the petitioner amounts to an infraction of Article 16 (1) and (2) of the Constitution, which guarantee equality to all in matters of public employment, regardless of religion, caste, sex, descent, place of birth, residence etc. A seemingly "neutral" reason such as inability of the employee, or unwillingness, if not probed closely, would act in a discriminatory manner, directly impacting her service rights. That is exactly what has happened here: though CRPF asserts that seniority benefit at par with the petitioner's colleagues and batchmates (who were able to clear course No. 85) cannot be given to her because she did not attend that course, in truth, her "unwillingness" stemmed from her inability due to her pregnancy . . . That the petitioner exercised her right therefore to become a parent should not operate to penalize her, and her choice to do so was irrelevant, in the circumstances of the case; the CRPF should have taken the reasons for the unwillingness into account given the admitted fact that she was pregnant.[8]

The Supreme Court of India, in *Lt Col Nitisha & Ors v. Union of India & Ors*[9] which deservedly is discussed in a separate chapter in this book, dealing with promotions to officers of the army, endorsed the decision of the Delhi

High Court delivered in *Ravina* case, where it is observed that while challenges of employment may seem to be perfectly neutral, in reality they might adversely impact one gender more than the other.

Indirect Discrimination and Substantive Equality

The decision delivered by the Delhi High Court in *Ravina* and the subsequent endorsement of the same by the Supreme Court of India in *Nitisha* highlights the relationship between indirect discrimination towards women in the workspace and the concept of substantive equality as has been studied by feminist theorists and writers since the 1970s. The Supreme Court of India in the above landmark decision closely inspected and observed that the doctrine of substantive equality and anti-stereotyping has been a critical evolution of the Indian Constitutional jurisprudence on Article 14 and 15(1). The Supreme Court of India also relied upon the decision in *Anuj Garg v. Hotel Association of India*[10] where it was held that sex-based discrimination is constitutionally impermissible and often acts as a barrier for women from enjoying full and equal citizenship.

The phenomenon of indirect discrimination was discussed by writer and academic Sandra Fredman, in her book *Human Rights Transformed: Positive Rights and Positive Duties* where she pertinently notes that 'treating people alike despite pre-existing disadvantages or discrimination can simply perpetuate inequality'.[11] The concept of substantive equality often revolves around recognizing differences rather than forcing symmetry and furthers the view that everyone must not only have the right to participate but also have the ability along with the resources to exercise this right. This is essential if we wish to ensure that laws and policies do not have a discriminatory effect.

A similarity between the decisions delivered by the constitutional courts in *Ravina* and *Nitisha* case is the manner in which the courts have distinguished the intention behind a practice or policy from the impact of the same. In relation to this, the courts succinctly observed that while a policy or practice may not intend to be discriminatory, the impact of the same may simply be, owing to 'unconscious/implicit biases or an inability to recognize how existing structures/institutions, and ways of doing things, have the consequence of freezing an unjust *status quo*'.[12] In both the judgments, the courts have resonated that systematic discrimination against women is antithetical to ensuring substantive equality. These lines from the decision in *Nitisha* summarize the spirit of this discussion aptly:

> The duty of constitutional courts when confronted with such a scheme of things, would not just be to strike down the discriminatory practices and compensate for the harm hitherto arising out of them; but also structure adequate reliefs and remedies that facilitate social redistribution by providing positive entitlement that aim to negate the scope of future harm.[13]

Conclusion

While the Delhi High Court restored the seniority, pay and dignity of Assistant Commandant Ravina, and allowed her petition directing for consequential seniority at par with her batchmates, fixation of pay and arrears of pay to her, there are millions of women across the globe who find themselves grappling with such battles and conundrums on a daily basis. Often, this kind of discrimination is perceived as facially neutral. The absence of availability of a constitutional remedy against such indirect discrimination in the corporate and private sectors allows these practices to propagate in dangerous proportions across workplaces. This case before the Delhi High Court is a good example to elucidate that what is seemingly benign is a far greater malaise.

As professionals and mothers from different generations, we have traversed this path ourselves and can vouch with some responsibility that it is excruciating and devastating for any woman to come to a crossroad where she has to choose between having a child or a career. Why does it have to be one at the expense of another? Pregnancy and maternity are often equated to disability or unwillingness. What is at stake is not just jeopardizing the participation of one half of the population of the world towards community building, but the very existence and well-being of our future generations. Unless we are ready to put the progress of humankind in reverse gear, regressing from scientific temper and innovation to the Stone Age, we have to do much more as a civilization. In stable and progressive democracies, with constitutional recognition of basic human rights, rule of law and an independent judiciary, most of these battles are not bloody. However, as the modem world finds itself coiling and recoiling, over and over again, on the contours of women's right of reproductive choice, it is all the more imperative that we see the preservation and exercise of this fundamental right as an asset, rather than a liability to the nations and humanity itself. The power of being a woman must be seen as a coveted position of status rather than some disqualification.

7

Leading the Charge or Lagging Behind?

Captain Loveleen Kaur Mann

State v. Air Force Administrative College

What I fear most is power with impunity. I fear abuse of power, and the power to abuse.

—Isabel Allende

Harassment at the workplace is devastating for any person who endures it. When we speak of sexual harassment, it is not only distressing for the victim but also reaffirms traditional gender roles rooted in a culture that, put bluntly, views women as inferior to men. The bedrock of India's legal framework, the Constitution, unequivocally guarantees the foundational right of gender equality. Enshrined within its provisions, notably Articles 14, 15 and 21, is the recognition that sexual harassment constitutes a detrimental infringement upon a woman's inherent right to equality. Moreover, constitutional provisions affirm the entitlement to a secure environment devoid of harassment for women. The Supreme Court of India has acknowledged that sexual harassment at the workplace is a glaring human rights violation time and again and the government has also taken steps to officially address it through a handbook.[1]

This essay delves into the issue of sexual harassment within the confines of the Indian Armed Forces, spotlighting the glaring chasm between the statutory framework provided by the Sexual Harassment at Workplace (Prevention, Prohibition and Redressal) Act, 2013 (PoSH Act)[2] and its actual implementation. Central to this examination is the exploration of the experiences, representation and acknowledgment of women within the military, which embodies a critical aspect of gender parity. Many women from diverse backgrounds are drawn towards military service by a profound sense of duty and patriotism, taking the same solemn oath as their male comrades-in-arms. Though not rampant, yet regrettably for some, this noble pursuit transforms into a harrowing ordeal as they confront sexual harassment within the ostensibly secure and inclusive precincts of their military units and installations.

The Gender Power Dynamics and Law

The term 'sexual harassment' was coined in the year 1970.[3] Over the past few decades, several notable feminist theorists have linked this phenomenon in the workspace as rooted in discrimination, power, privilege and sex-based inequality.[4]

Power is centric to any discussion surrounding sexual harassment in the workplace. Addressing this imbalance in the power dynamics between men and women, the apex judicial body in India, the Supreme Court, laid down what came to be known as the *Vishaka Guidelines* in 1997 in absence of a direct substantive statute on the subject.[5] Sexual harassment, as defined by the Supreme Court of India in this landmark judgment, refers to unwelcome, direct and indirect sexually determined behaviour which includes within its ambit: (a) physical contact and advances, (b) demand or request for sexual favours, (c) sexually coloured remarks, (d) showing pornography or (e) any other unwelcome physical, verbal or non-verbal conduct of sexual nature.[6] Indian constitutional courts have clarified as to what constitutes 'sexual harassment' over time. In the case of *Shanta Kumar v. Council of Scientific and Industrial Research (CDIR) & Ors*,[7] the court clarified that not all physical forms of contact by a man towards a woman can be construed as sexual harassment. The court further observed that it is crucial to gauge the undertone and intent of sexual nature to qualify a physical advance as sexual harassment (in comparison with mere harassment).[8]

The harmful impact of sexual harassment in the workplace cannot be overstated, as it fosters an atmosphere of insecurity and hostility that dissuades women from active participation in the workforce, thereby impeding their social and economic advancement. After the *Vishaka Guidelines*, India enacted its first legislation addressing sexual harassment in the workplace—the PoSH Act in the year 2013, thereby rendering statutory basis to the issues flagged by the Supreme Court of India.

The *Vishaka Guidelines* provided a clear definition of sexual harassment and were revolutionary as they laid down an extensive framework to prevent such cases. The guidelines also created a complaint mechanism to put in place a time-bound processing of complaints and also provided for disciplinary action where such conduct was to be treated at par with 'misconduct in employment' which was, in turn, to be defined by the relevant service rules, as reiterated recently by the Supreme Court.[9] Both *Vishaka Guidelines* and the PoSH Act firmly place the onus on employers, for preventing and deterring sexual harassment at workplace[10] as well as taking all the necessary steps to thoroughly investigate and effectively deal with complaints about such torment, including prosecution when it is called for under the law. The PoSH Act lists ten different and wide-ranging 'duties of the employer' that are aimed at ensuring a safe and secure workplace for women. For this essay, it is essential to point out that the *Vishaka Guidelines* required the formation of 'Internal Complaint Committees' against sexual harassment at workplaces.

As is evident from a brief synopsis of the legal landscape in India, there is a call to fix accountability in such matters. However, as has been recently observed by the Supreme Court of India, even after *Vishaka Guidelines* of 1997 and the PoSH Act in 2013, the simplest requirements concerning formation of an Internal Complaints Committee have not effectively seen the light of day in several organizations.[11]

A perusal of the facts of the present case under discussion paints a grim picture—these requirements were left unfulfilled and were ignored with impunity by an organization entrusted with the safety and security of an entire nation, and it is in that light that a constitutional court took note of the situation.

From a sociological perspective, the requirement to ensure safety of women in the workplace and especially prevent sexual harassment has been touched upon in several notable studies. In one such attempt, which was a survey conducted by three sociologists, interviews from a Youth Development Study were analysed. The study found how 'power-threat' theory makes women in positions of authority frequent targets.[12] An interesting observation made in this study was that aspects such as gender nonconformity and consequent social isolation in the workplace where there exists an unbalanced sex ratio affects the possibility for such an unfortunate set of circumstances to thrive. The case discussed in this essay and the treatment meted out to the victim is a classic example of what has been described as 'hegemonic masculinity' by the sociologist Raewyn Connell who argued that society holds a 'single normative ideal' for men and male behaviour, which in turn determines the broad sociological framework concerning harassment, gender and power.[13]

The Case

In the present case, *State represented by the Inspector of Police v. Commandant, Air Force Administrative College*,[14] heard by a bench of the Madras High Court presided by Justice R.N. Manjula, the de-facto complainant and the accused were flight lieutenants in the Indian Air Force (equivalent to the rank of captain of the army). Both the parties were undergoing a Professional Knowledge Course for seven weeks at the Air Force Administrative College (AFAC), Coimbatore, from 16 August 2021 to 9 September 2021. As per the complainant, she retreated to her accommodation after an evening party at the Officers' Mess in AFAC on the night intervening 9 September 2021 and 10 September 2021. The room was thereafter locked from outside by another coursemate of hers. The de-facto complainant was unconscious and could not offer resistance when the accused allegedly trespassed into her room at 12.30 a.m. on 10 September 2021 and sexually assaulted her. What followed, as per her, was mistreatment meted out to the victim who was not only humiliated during the medical examination at the military hospital but was also coerced to withdraw the complaint on two occasions by senior officers. What is rather shocking is the fact that the evidence collected from the place of occurrence was not sent for forensic examination till 23 September 2021, and the accused was allowed to sit in classes alongside the victim for such a time period. It was only after the victim chose to prefer a police complaint on 20 September 2021 and registered a case under Section 376(1) of the Indian Penal Code (IPC) that matters were finally taken up as they should have from the very beginning when the act was reported to the AFAC authorities.

The local police initiated the investigation by visiting the AFAC premises, taking the accused into custody for producing him before a judicial magistrate. At this point, Indian Air Force authorities sought custody of the accused under Section 124 of Air Force Act, 1950 read with Section 475 Code of Criminal Procedure (CrPC) and the Criminal Courts and Court Martial (Adjustment of Jurisdiction) Rules, 1978, which was granted by the magistrate. The local police petitioned before the Madras High Court that the handing over the accused to the authorities of the Air Force was premature. The police argued that the Acts and Rules cited were applicable only when the chargesheet was filed and the cognizance was taken by the magistrate. A petition was thus preferred by the police to address the legal conundrum. The respondent, Indian Air Force, submitted before the Madras High Court that the accused was ultimately tried by a court martial and convicted for the offence, therefore, the criminal petition became infructuous. Furthermore, it was argued by the Indian Air Force that the accused was detained and arrested by the police authorities in an illegal manner in contravention of the law.

The Indian Armed Forces personnel are subject to specific Army, Naval and Air Force Acts that spell out offences to be tried by court martial. These statutes are to be read along with the IPC, Indian Evidence Act and the CrPC—the exceptional offences being murder, culpable homicide not amounting to murder and rape, which can only be tried by criminal courts while the other offences can be tried either in regular courts or court martial. In the present case, the victim (woman officer) as well as the accused were both subject to Section 2(a) of the Air Force Act, 1950. She chose to submit a police complaint for sexual assault under Section of 376(1) of the IPC simply due to the inadequate manner in which the AFAC authorities were carrying out the investigation once she had reported it. This set of circumstances would have been different if an Internal Complaints Committee as envisaged in the *Vishaka Guidelines* as well as the safeguards provided in the PoSH Act had been effectively put in place by the Indian Air Force.

While discussing the reasons as to why the de-facto complainant chose to prefer a complaint before the police in the first place, the Madras High Court in its decision observed:

> . . . the necessity to register a case by the police arose due to the complaint filed by the victim. Having not [been] satisfied with the way in which the things were handled by Air Force authorities subsequent to her reporting and having faced humiliation and threat to withdraw the complaint, the victim had approached the police.[15]

The Indian Armed Forces are based on meritocracy. As men and women, we all start out on the same playing field with the same oath. The moot point here is that a woman who serves the armed forces as an equal partner in both mental robustness and endurance, does not get the opportunity and support to fight the crime of rape or sexual assault as a victim. Rather, at times, she faces humiliation at the hands of doctors who examine her as well as fellow comrades who have taken the oath to share camaraderie with her. Obviously, today's military is much more integrated along gender lines than at any time in the past and is also sensitive to such issues. In view of the same, it is imperative to ensure a safe and secure workplace free from sexual harassment towards women with the armed forces being at the forefront, just as they appreciably are in many different facets of society.

Madras High Court's Observations on the Internal Complaints Committee

A crucial aspect of the PoSH Act is the establishment of an Internal Complaints Committee within organizations to encourage reporting and accountability. The committee serves as a platform where personnel can safely report incidents of harassment without fear of retaliation. By providing a confidential and supportive space for reporting, the PoSH Act ensures that incidents are promptly addressed, and the perpetrators are held accountable. This increased accountability in turn promotes a workplace where gender equity is respected and upheld. In this case, the Madras High Court directed:

> . . . the Central government is directed to ensure the proper existence of Internal Complaints Committee

in the Armed Forces in accordance with the mandate of the Sexual Harassment of Women at Workplace (Prevention, Prohibition and Redressal) Act 2013 and to sensitize the armed personnel by imparting gender sensitive awareness training to achieve its objectives.[16]

The Madras High Court further directed the Ministry of Defence to implement the PoSH Act in the Indian Armed Forces. Such a direction from a court has been long overdue as none of the defence services (army, navy or air force) have effectively implemented the provisions of the PoSH Act. The implementation has remained notional. Under the PoSH Act, it is mandatory for the employer to treat sexual harassment as 'misconduct' under the service rules, therefore, the matter can be investigated as per the due process laid down in the service rules without a written complaint from the victim, and post investigation, due action can be taken by the employer.

The Indian courts have elaborated on what an Internal Complaints Committee can and cannot do. In the 2018 case of *Shital Prasad Sharma v. State of Rajasthan & Ors*,[17] the Rajasthan High Court clarified that a committee could initiate an investigation on the basis of a complaint forwarded or received by other sources of authority as long as the complainant agrees to take the matter forward with them. In *Sarita Verma v. New Delhi Municipal Corporation & Ors*,[18] the Delhi High Court clarified that a committee must not halt or end its investigation if the complainant chooses to initiate parallel proceedings with any other forum for redressal. The committee has to independently conduct its investigation as per the due process of the law.

In the matter of *M. Rajendran v. Daisyrani & Ors*,[19] the Madras High Court provided clarity on maintaining the impartial and unbiased investigative approach during the proceedings. It further stated if individual members of the committee investigating a certain matter are under the supervision or direct authority of either of the parties, an impartial and fair investigation is difficult to achieve. In *Gaurav Jain v. Hindustan Latex Family Planning Promotion Trust & Ors*,[20] the Delhi High Court stated that sexual harassment at the workplace can also mean a hostile and oppressive work environment for a woman employee when power and authority from a male member of the organization are being used to force her to accompany him on his outstation travels and late-night meetings.

The Madras High Court also emphasized on sensitizing the armed forces personnel by imparting gender sensitive awareness training to achieve its objectives and comply with PoSH Act.

A few recommendations are in order:

(i) **Gender Sensitivity: Laying the Foundation for Inclusivity**

At the heart of promoting gender equality is gender sensitivity. Organizations play a significant role in fostering a healthy safe and secure place for their employees, and the absence of a framework to prevent sexual harassment does enable sexual violence.[21] Gender sensitivity training plays a vital role in raising awareness about unconscious biases, stereotypes and discriminatory practices that might unintentionally perpetuate gender disparities. Through regular gender sensitivity workshops, Indian Armed Forces can sensitize employees to the impact of their language, behaviour and actions on colleagues of different genders. This training fosters empathy and understanding, creating an environment where everyone feels valued and included, regardless of their gender identity. This also somewhere a sensitized leadership can also assist since it is often the case that organization leadership can significantly enhance 'institutional courage' by pushing for a better workspace for all.[22]

(ii) **PoSH Training: Empowering Armed Forces Personnel with Knowledge**

In workspaces where sexual harassment is not taken seriously, it is more likely to occur.[23] Many sociologists and psychologists have theorized that the only way to reverse the negative or hostile work atmosphere created due to gender discrimination is by intensive counter-stereotypical training.[24] PoSH training is a critical component of effectively implementing the PoSH Act. This training would equip armed forces personnel with the knowledge and understanding of what constitutes sexual harassment, how to recognize it and the appropriate steps to be undertaken when faced with such situations. When personnel undergo PoSH training, they become active participants in promoting a safe and respectful workplace. They learn to identify and report incidents of harassment promptly, contributing to the prevention and deterrence of such behaviour. PoSH training empowers them with the confidence to take a stand against harassment, creating a collective commitment to gender equality.

(iii) **PoSH Awareness: Building a Culture of Accountability**
A key factor in promoting gender equality is also building a culture of accountability. When it is evident to members of an organization that the approach of their organization is lenient towards sexual harassment, they may not fear the consequences of the same and assume that anyone who does report it would be disregarded and to an extent even penalized.[25] PoSH awareness initiatives within the Indian Armed Forces would play a pivotal role in this regard. Regular communication and dissemination of information related to the PoSH Act ensure that both leadership and personnel are aware of their rights and responsibilities. Armed forces personnel should know how to access the Internal Complaints Committee if they experience or witness any incident of sexual harassment. PoSH awareness campaigns, workshops and posters serve as reminders of the organization's commitment to a safe and respectful workplace for all.

An important observation by the Madras High Court that highlights the plight of the victim in the present case and reiterates importance of an Internal Complaints Committee is as under:

> In this era of awareness and sensitivity, it is difficult to comprehend that a victim of a sexual offence in the armed forces was not comfortable enough to take up her grievance and she was looked down [upon] and pressured for having got the courage to report. If the women of the armed forces should not have courage to fight such violence, who else can have?[26]

Counter Stereotypical Roles and Sexual Harassment

Individuals who face sexual harassment are often challenging the stereotypical norms perpetuated by the society at large. Sexual harassment might not be just a result of sexual desire, and if it were the case, most individuals who fell victim to it would be those who met the so-called 'gender ideals' set by the society.[27] Contrary to this belief, many psychologists have found that it is very common for sexual harassment in the workplace to take place towards persons who sway away from the gender ideals set by society.[28] One can gather from the facts of the case under discussion, as well as the decision delivered, that the contributing social and psychological factors leading to the offence in the first place, as well as the conduct of the AFAC authorities, is rooted in how unprepared the institution was to address an unfortunately common situation for which the law is already settled and safeguards are in place. The increasing number of women in the armed forces presents a deviation from the social norm that has been found to be one of the major triggers for gender-based harassment.[29] One study found that a reason why male workers often harass women in a workplace where women are breaking gender norms is usually because they are motivated to act in such ways to 'derogate women when they experience a threat to their male identity'.[30]

Gender minorities often face the risk of sexual harassment in a job where they may be viewed as outsiders or where their occupation is counter stereotypical.[31] At present, it is undeniable that while the number of women in the armed forces is steadily and surely rising due to new opportunities and gateways being opened for them, but they are still a gender minority. The risk of harassment is thus higher for women in such a workplace.[32] As a result, it is imperative that legal safeguards, which have proven themselves to be essential in every workspace, be adopted in both letter and spirit by the Indian Armed Forces which undeniably have disproportionate gender ratios.

Conclusion

While the share of women in the Indian Armed Forces is higher than ever, the experiences of women in the military are often inequitable. Some women in the military suffer sexual harassment and the incidents, many a time, are followed by pressure from senior officials and general insensitivity where the attitude leans towards saving the face of the organization rather than ensuring that the victim's concerns are redressed. This gap in redressal of real and genuine problems impeding women's participation in such jobs could be addressed by effectively implementing the PoSH Act in the Indian Armed Forces as statutorily envisaged and ensuring its compliance as well as sensitizing personnel by imparting gender sensitivity awareness training, as, of course, already rightly stated by the Madras High Court. If we are to eventually see equal share of men and women in the Indian Armed Forces, and *nari shakti* (female power) in full force, this is imperative and a serious need of the hour.

Organizations that proactively implement the PoSH Act demonstrate their commitment to providing a safe and equitable work environment. The defence services are accurately thought of as being one of the most righteous organizations with a great deal of trust reposed by the public, and it is time to analyse if we are leading the way to eliminate gender-based discrimination or lagging behind other institutions. It is essential to remind ourselves that we are living and breathing in 2024. The *Vishaka Guidelines* have been in place since 1997, the PoSH Act since 2013, if these provisions are not practically and temporally implemented now, then when?

8

Challenging Bias and Gender Narratives

Ratna Viswanathan

Balvinder Kaur v. Union of India

In the silent corridors of justice,
the clang of discrimination echoes loudly.

—Bell Hooks[1]

History is replete with instances of women who have navigated a labyrinth of barriers and biases to carve out their rightful place in professions that are traditionally dominated by men, and these poignant words by Hooks resonate profoundly against the complex tapestry of timeless struggle for gender equality. The case of *Balvinder Kaur v. Union of India*[2] illustrates another significant instance of this unending struggle, highlighting the endemic and deeply entrenched inequalities women in uniform continue to endure. Yet, they courageously keep fighting and winning these battles of a different nature against all odds.

Balvinder Kaur joined the Military Nursing Service (MNS) as a lieutenant on 1 June 1988 and married Captain Y.K. Joseph on 31 December 1988, while still on probation. Consequently, her services were terminated on 23 October 1989, since marriage during probation was in violation of a stipulation in the applicable rules ordaining prohibition on marriage during probation. In 1995, Balvinder Kaur filed a writ petition before the Delhi High Court against the Union of India on the premise of violation of Articles 15 and 16 of the Constitution of India, challenging the unfair rules that restricted her from marrying while on probation as a trainee.

Under the rules, this ban on marriage was purportedly imposed because it was felt by the military firmament that if MNS officers married during probation, they would in turn probably get pregnant and would proceed to be on long leave as was due to them, thus not deriving the benefit of training for the entire probation period. Articles 15 and 16 prohibit discrimination against women and they also give the State the power to accord positive discrimination in favour of women under the right conditions. But ironically, the extant instance was in contradiction of these provisions.

Interestingly, the role of women in the Indian armed forces, which can be traced to 1888, when India was still under British rule, commenced with the setting up of the Indian Military Nursing Service. The Indian Military Nursing Service was statutorily categorized as an 'armed force'. It is telling that despite being the first cadre of women officers in the armed forces, even today they face gender discrimination due to archaic rules based on unsustainable suppositions.

The ban on marriage during probation for MNS officers, ostensibly justified by concerns of potential pregnancy and disrupted training, symbolized institutional bias rooted in an outdated perception of female capabilities. The pivotal role of women in the Indian armed forces dates back to the late nineteenth century, and yet, even as on this date, discriminatory rules continue to create hurdles on their path to gender equality in the forces. The proverbial glass ceiling is not a myth but a distressing reality that keeps getting reinforced.

A brief reading of the factual aspects of the case reveals that Balvinder Kaur's marriage was treated as being violative of a service criterion titled 'Clause A' that stated that an MNS officer who married during probation would not be retained in service. Consequently, her services were terminated. Interestingly, MNS officers are all women so the counter question of whether Clause A applied to all genders is redundant in this instance. Balvinder Kaur challenged both Clause A of the service order as well as her termination from service, citing it as being discriminatory as well as being in violation of Articles 15 and 16 of the Constitution of India. Article 15 mentions prohibition of discrimination on the grounds of religion, race, caste, sex or place of birth and Article 16 mentions equality of opportunity in matters of public employment.

The contention of Balvinder Kaur was that her termination was discriminatory, and the court upheld her petition stating that the flawed assumption that marriage would lead to pregnancy and hence the probation period would reduce to a period of eleven months as opposed to the stipulated twenty-four months as the probationer would proceed on maternity leave, was based on a premise and not fact. Balvinder Kaur should have been provided the opportunity to prove that marriage was not a handicap. Justice Usha Mehra, who heard the matter, ruled that the order flowed out of a bias on account of the sex (gender) of the petitioner and was violative of Articles 15 and 16. In any event, the petitioner would not have been automatically confirmed but would have been judged on performance and then confirmed and that was the only criterion that mattered.[3] Previously, there had been a blanket ban on marriage for MNS officers. This had subsequently been withdrawn in 1968. However, it still applied to the probation period of MNS officers. The court held that there was little difference in the blanket ban on marriage for women in the MNS while in service and a ban during the probation period as both were based on the gender of the officer.

While the petitioner argued against the ban, citing various rulings by constitutional courts that deemed blanket bans on women's marriage unconstitutional, she also emphasized the need for equality of opportunity in employment as enshrined in Articles 15 and 16 of the Indian Constitution. The respondent acknowledged the withdrawal of the blanket ban on marriage but sought to justify the prohibition during the probationary period by highlighting the imagined concerns of the establishment over reduced probationary periods due to maternity leave.

Historically, MNS officers have had to deal with a long-standing prohibition on marriage, purportedly due to concerns over women's domestic commitments acting as an impediment to their efficient performance of duties. However, this stance was challenged in the Kerala High Court in the case of *Lt (MNS) M.M. Sujaya, INHS v. Director General Military Nursing Service & Ors*[4] that deemed such discrimination unconstitutional under Articles 14, 15 and 16. The court reasoned that similar concerns over domestic commitments exist for male doctors and (civilian) nurses in Armed Forces Hospitals, yet they were not subject to the same restrictions. Drawing parallels with previous legal precedents, the court rejected the argument that marriage during the probationary period automatically diminishes a woman's ability to perform her duties effectively.

In the case of Balvinder Kaur, the Delhi High Court reproduced the extracts of an earlier decision of the Supreme Court in the *Indira Kumari Kartiayani v. The Maha Nideshak, Raksha Mantralaya, Shastra Sena Chikitsa Seva* in the judgment:

> It is not disputed that, but for the marriage, the appellant's performance would have been of sufficiently good average to be retained in service and to be considered for promotion to the next higher post on the basis of her

seniority . . . her service had to be discontinued because of the marriage coupled with the fact that she had not obtained high efficiency performance rate during the three years preceding the marriage. The Additional Solicitor General appearing for the respondent submitted that with a view to guaranteeing the efficiency of the MNS that it was decided that after marriage a person could remain in service only if she justified her continuance by showing extra efficiency in the years preceding marriage. What was ordinarily good enough for continuing in service was not good enough once a person was married. She could remain in service notwithstanding the general rule of termination on marriage, by showing extra ability in the past to assure the authorities of her ability to perform well in the future despite marriage.[5]

The Delhi High Court emphasized the principles of natural justice, asserting that women officers should be given the chance to demonstrate their ability to balance marriage and professional responsibilities. The court dismissed the presumption that marriage inevitably leads to reduced probationary periods, highlighting the arbitrary nature of such assumptions, by observing that:

> . . . the alleged presumption of the respondent that on account of marriage in each and every case of probation the period would get reduced to 11 months as against 24 months, is nothing but the figment of the respondent's imagination . . .[6]

Ultimately, the court set aside the order terminating the petitioner's service, emphasizing that termination should only occur if a woman fails to meet performance standards during the probationary period. The judgment reaffirms the constitutional guarantee of equality of opportunity in employment and condemns discriminatory practices that undermine women's rights in the workplace. The high court recorded:

> The petitioner's service could only be terminated if it had been the case of the respondent that she did not complete the probation period satisfactorily or that her performance was not good or that she was inefficient.[7]

This judgment had parallels with what the Supreme Court had observed in the case of an Indian Foreign Service officer, *C.B. Muthamma v. Union Of India*, '. . . sex prejudice against the Indian womanhood pervades the service rules even a third of a century after Freedom . . .'[8]

The Supreme Court in the said case analysed individual rules of service and found that:

> If a woman member shall obtain the permission of Government before the marriage, the same risk is run by Government if a male member contracts a marriage. If the family and domestic commitments of a woman member of the service is likely to come in the way of efficient discharge of duties, a similar situation may well arise in the case of a male member . . . If a married man

has a right, a married woman, other things being equal, stands on no worse footing. Freedom is indivisible, so is justice.[9]

While the cases of *Balvinder Kaur*, *C.B. Muthamma*, *Vishaka*[10] (this case led to the *Vishaka Guidelines*, defining sexual harassment and placing the onus on employers to provide a safe working environment for women), *Mary Roy v. State of Kerala*[11] (where the Supreme Court granted Syrian Christian women the right to seek an equal share in their father's property) and *Lata Singh v. State of Uttar Pradesh*[12] (the court upheld an adult woman's right to marry or live with anyone of her choice) are iconic decisions and have sought to bring in equality, the bias, subconscious or otherwise, is so deeply engrained that it is difficult to move beyond stereotyping. To quote Simone de Beauvoir, the French writer, philosopher and feminist, 'If I want to define myself, I first have to say, "I am a woman"; all other assertions will arise from this basic truth. A man never begins by positing himself as an individual of a certain sex: that he is a man is obvious.'[13]

This chapter has no doubt emerged from the inequality women face in the forces, but it reflects what has evolved and played out in the larger societal context. The origin of gender stereotypes dates back to the division of roles in early human societies which typically derived from biological differences and were functional. What they also did was reinforce men's strength and women's nurturing abilities. By the time agriculture evolved and societies became more sedentary, these roles crystallized further and became more rigid. Men continued to engage in harder physical labour and women managed the household. It is interesting how, with every iteration of progress, these roles became more and more embedded. The Industrial Revolution had men working in mines, construction and factories while women worked in less physically demanding jobs such as in textile mills or households. And this pattern pretty much reflected right up to the World Wars. There, as the men went to war, women had to take over roles traditionally handled by them for the first time, but were expected to go back to their original roles once the wars were over.

Closer home, during the Vedic Age, women enjoyed considerable rights and had a significant standing in the social order.[14] However, by around 500 BCE, these rights began to erode. Women were gradually denied the *Upanayana Sanskara*, the Hindu rite of passage that marks a boy's entrance into the world of Vedas and his readiness to perform rituals, which had previously given them access to education. As a result, they were excluded from formal learning.[15] The advent of purdah[16] and the influence of successive invaders further marginalized women, both in public and private spheres.[17] Around 200 CE, the *Manusmriti* institutionalized these changes, with edicts such as 'By a girl, by a young woman or even an aged one, nothing must be done independently,'[18] reinforcing rigid societal expectations. Over time, these restrictions solidified into the norms we see being challenged even today.

In the mid-twentieth century, the women's liberation movement fought against these long-standing gender biases, demanding equal access to education, employment, and leadership roles.[19] Despite these efforts, stereotypes about women's competence, commitment and leadership skills continue to affect workplace dynamics. These biases can manifest subtly, in the form of microaggressions—such as offhand remarks about assertiveness or concerns over childcare leave—or more overtly, through systemic barriers like limited career advancement opportunities.

These reactions, subtle or otherwise, shape women's career trajectories, often diverting them from positions they deserve. Recognizing and addressing these nuanced biases is crucial for fostering true gender equality.

As far as the armed forces are concerned, in 2020 the Supreme Court of India issued a landmark judgment in the *Babita Puniya*[20] case wherein it ruled that Permanent Commission (PC) be granted to women officers who had been serving under the Short Service Commission (SSC) scheme. The judgment came in the wake of a case filed by women officers who had served for fourteen years and were denied a PC by the army. Women already serve in combat roles in the air force, and as for the navy, an in-principle decision has been taken that women officers will soon be permitted to serve on ships and submarines. In the army, women officers are already serving in combat components such as the sappers and the artillery and have been inducted in the ranks for the Corps of Military Police.

While there is a perceptible shift in the role of women in the forces, put into motion no doubt by the landmark decision of the Supreme Court on PC among others, there are discussions around the infrastructure to cater to women's needs, acceptance of women leaders by troops in combat roles due to deeply embedded patriarchy and vulnerability to sexual harassment. Patriarchy and sexual harassment, however, are not limited to women serving in the forces. These issues are similarly relevant in non-military environments too. So, the argument over the years that women cannot be deployed in combat roles seems more like men guarding what they perceive to be their turf. Although women have now been granted permanency in line with the ruling of the Supreme Court of India, they are still not deployed in proper combat roles. To state fairly, several countries like Russia, the United States and even Israel have women serving the military, but the jury is still out on whether they should be deployed in combat roles or not. Interestingly, in a country like Israel, where one assumes that there are equal roles for men and women, they are restricted from assault forces and elite units.

According to 2022 data,[21] the number of women in the army was 3.97 per cent of the total strength, it was 6 per cent of the total strength of the navy and in the air force, it was 13.69 per cent. On a pan-India level, women in the workforce as of 2022 data stood at 27.98 per cent, and by October 2023, it had reached 37 per cent. This upward trend in women's participation in the workforce is a healthy sign and one expects that the armed forces will reflect a similar positive movement in terms of women joining.

To come back to the issue of women and their roles in the forces, much has been said about women in combat versus non-combat roles. The obvert and subconscious biases that play a big part in this cannot be wished away, as they evolve from a masculine subculture embedded in our socialization processes. Women have done very well in what were previously perceived male bastions and have effectively increased the talent pool available to any sector. As a result of the same masculine subculture that looks at sympathy and empathy as being signs of weakness, women bring in these traits that can ease potentially explosive situations. In this context, the publication by Deepanjali Bakshi, *In the Line of Fire: Women in the Indian Armed Forces*,[22] is worth reading. Formerly from the Indian Army, Deepanjali had the opportunity of having a ringside view of what it means to be a woman officer. She contends that even after years from when women have been inducted into the armed forces, very little has changed for them in terms of career opportunities and exposure. Since mostly men hold a position of authority, their preconceived notions about the capabilities of a woman officer often lead to their limiting the role of women. For the women who join the services however, it is a serious career option, and they have the same aspirations and career goals as men. There is a need to understand this aspiration better and look at women from a lens of capability rather than gender, since by doing so, their potential becomes limited.

To quote from Bakshi's paper, 'The connection between the military and masculinity is an enduring one. Military service has long been a masculine rite of passage where boys become men after joining the military. All Armed Forces unabashedly play on this sentiment to swell their rank and file – "join the Army, be a man", "the Army will make a man out of you", "we're looking for a few good men" and many such others. This calling of men is perceived as a challenge to their masculinity with all its associated values of aggression, strength and combativeness. For women to be accepted in this scheme of things raises questions about men's very identity, as women are traditionally viewed as the weak collective "other", who must be kept out of all rites and traditions of the military. The argument for the exclusion of women from the army then is based not on their inherent desire for peace, but because they are imbued with insufficient masculinity.'

Going forward, it is important to focus on this particular nuance and to not undermine the seriousness and aspiration of women coming into the defence services. Looking at women through purely a physiological lens dilutes what they consider a serious career option. It is important that women be assessed in the light of their abilities and not their gender. Let them be subject to uniform standards of training and recruitment, and if they qualify, they should be treated in the same way as their male counterparts. Though there will always be a few good men and women, like *Balvinder Kaur*, fighting for the cause of justice, the voice of equality needs to emanate from within the system rather than from those who opt to take a stand, or as a result of judicial intervention. Interestingly, while Balvinder Kaur's case was decided way back in the year 1995, it was in 2024 that it found a soul-sister in the decision of the Supreme Court in *Union of India v. Ex Lt Selina John* wherein the court, while dealing with the case of an MNS officer released from service on account of her marriage, termed the said rule as 'ex-facie manifestly arbitrary, as terminating employment because the woman has got married is a coarse case of gender discrimination and inequality', further stating that 'acceptance of such patriarchal rule undermines human dignity, right to non-discrimination and fair treatment.' [23]

The key issue is one of fairness, dignity and equality. As Justice Ruth Bader Ginsburg of the Supreme Court of the United States powerfully articulated, 'Women belong in all places where decisions are being made. It shouldn't be that women are the exception.' [24] These words are a profound call to action, and the armed forces would do well to make this an integral part of their approach to recruitment and career progression for women in the forces. The strength in the so-called soft skills that women bring add a powerful dimension to conflict resolution that can be ill-ignored. With the nature of conflict morphing from pure physical engagement to far different means of engagement, the focus needs to shift on capability, adaptability and prowess rather than gender. It really is time to march ahead.

9

The Conundrum of Choice

Anu Pal

Captain (Mrs) Krishna v. Union of India

Because to take away a man's freedom of choice,
even his freedom to make the wrong choice,
is to manipulate him as though he were a puppet and not a
person.

—Madeline L'Engle

Gender roles have existed across cultures. The woman's role, in particular, was primarily restricted to focusing on the household and children. It was not deemed necessary for them to be educated or come out in public. However, things changed and along came extraordinary women who defied sociocultural norms, paving the way for future generations. One is left awe-inspired reading about women across ages—be it the enigmatic Queen of the Nile, Cleopatra; Valentina Tereshkova, the first woman in

112

space; the first Indian-origin astronaut, Kalpana Chawla; the mathematician Katherine Johnson, who used her exceptional skills for flight paths of spacecrafts for NASA; C.J. Walker, the first female self-made millionaire in the United States; Katherine Graham, the first female CEO of a Fortune 500 company; Joan of Arc; Rani Laxmi Bai of Jhansi; etc. The list is long, and perhaps endless, given the innumerable women whose lives have not been chronicled but who managed to break through quite a few glass ceilings.

And in the midst of them all, one suddenly comes back to reality and reads about Captain (Mrs) Krishna who was fighting an altogether different battle—wanting to resign from the armed forces in an attempt to save her marriage.

Captain Krishna had got her Permanent Commission (PC) in the Military Nursing Service (MNS) of the Indian Army in June 2001. In December 2004, she got married and in 2005 she was blessed with a daughter. The place of her matrimonial home and the place of work were different, and after the birth of their daughter, her husband asked her to stay with him permanently and called upon her to resign from service. Three years later, in September 2008, her husband filed a petition for divorce. One of the grounds for the divorce was that the couple had agreed before marriage that Captain Krishna would resign from service. Her husband was aggrieved by the fact that she was not performing her matrimonial duties, that he had been deprived of wedded bliss and separated from his wife and daughter. He claimed that the separation had induced dejection and loneliness, and he was desperate to end this kind of an arrangement. It is in this backdrop that Captain Krishna submitted her resignation, wanting an opportunity to end the acrimony in her matrimonial life and avoiding divorce under any circumstances.

Ultimately, her request for resignation was rejected by the competent military authority. The rejection order referred to the divorce petition filed by her husband. It was mentioned that the reason for filing of the same was not merely the service of the nursing officer but also the ill-treatment towards her in-laws. The rejection order stated that her spouse had also alleged that she was least interested in staying with him. The authority came to the conclusion that even her resignation from service would not resolve their matrimonial disharmony, and hence, her request for resignation could not be acceded to.

It is against this rejection order that she had approached the Delhi High Court.[1] The bench, comprising Justices Gita Mittal and J.R. Midha, ultimately set aside the rejection order and directed the authority to reconsider her resignation.

Before delving into the various aspects dealt by the court, it would be prudent to observe here that the Indian judiciary has played a pivotal role in safeguarding the fundamental rights enshrined in the Indian Constitution and ensuring justice, equality and rule of law. And for women in the armed forces, the road has certainly not been smooth. This judgment is one of the many examples of how the Indian courts deftly navigate the intersectionality between existing social realities on one hand, and the imperative of changing times on the other, at the same moment ensuring that the core principles of the Constitution are upheld, and rather suited, to the needs of the people they govern.

One of the applicable instructions relied upon by Captain Krishna was that in case a nursing officer desires to retire prematurely or resign her commission, she may apply as per rules. In the said instructions, 'extreme compassionate grounds' on account of 'matrimonial disharmony' was one such available reason.

The first and foremost exercise undertaken by the court was to determine as to the nature of the right of the petitioner that would be involved. It was the contention of Captain Krishna, the petitioner, that by resigning her commission, she would be making an endeavour to preserve her family by dispelling the acrimony and discord in her matrimonial life. After alluding to innumerable international covenants and treaties, many of which India is also a signatory to, the court observed that all of them emphasize the importance of family and the recognition of the right to family as well as the protection of the family unit as a basic human right. The court further cited judicial precedent on how the Indian judiciary has always read international treaties and conventions into the interpretation of constitutional provisions and domestic laws. By observing that there is no legislation in the country on the question that arises in the said matter, the right recognized by international conventions would guide the consideration of the right of the petitioner. A conjoint reading of them, the court held, made it abundantly clear that they recognized the family to be a natural and fundamental unit of society, and that parties are under an obligation to take appropriate steps to ensure equality of rights and responsibilities of spouses to marriage and that the States are also under an obligation to recognize and accord the widest possible protection and assistance to the family as a natural and fundamental unit of society. The court further went on to hold that even though marriage as a right has not received statutory recognition in any legislation in India, the Indian courts have read it to be a part of Article 21 of the Constitution of India.[2]

The court also held that human dignity is considered an essential concomitant of the right to life under Article 21 of the Constitution of India. Quoting Justice Krishna Iyer, the court cited a Supreme Court judgment that held that the guarantee of human dignity forms part of our human culture.[3] A Delhi High Court judgment was also cited where it was observed that the constitutional protection of dignity recognizes a person as a free being who develops his or her body and mind as he or she sees fit. The court held that at the root of the dignity is the autonomy of the private will and a person's freedom of choice and affection, and that human dignity rests on recognition of the physical and spiritual integrity of the human being, his or her humanity, and value as a person, irrespective of the utility he or she can provide to others.[4]

In a nutshell, the court held that the right the petitioner was claiming—to cohabit with her family—was an essential part of her Fundamental Right to Life guaranteed to her, and after establishing this right, the court went on to further examine the proposition.

The court took note of a similar matter that had come up before the Delhi High Court, where a doctor with the Indian Army had knocked the doors of the high court against the rejection of his application to resign. To quote from the judgment:

> *An application for resignation may be rejected if it is not based on adequate and justifiable reasons. The overriding consideration is whether the officer's continuance in service for a specific period is necessary to meet exigencies in a service and alternative arrangements cannot be made. Even in such a case, the application for resignation cannot be rejected. It can only be held in abeyance.*[5]

Other examples also were cited where the court, in similar circumstances, had set aside the impugned rejection order and sent the matter back to the competent authority to consider the request for resignation afresh.

The court very rightly observed that the authorities themselves had framed a policy where matrimonial harmony was one of the stated reasons under the category of extreme compassionate grounds. The court observed that while rejecting the resignation application, the authorities should not have gone into the merits of the divorce petition, and as per their own guidelines, the mere fact of its existence was sufficient. Though of course, practically speaking, one cannot rule out that at times it may be a ruse in order to secure a resignation.

It was observed by the court that the rejection of the application to resign did not refer to non-availability of adequate manpower in the category of officers where the petitioner was employed. No exigency of service, let alone any extremity, was even suggested. The court recorded the claim of the petitioner that her husband had clearly indicated that she must resign from service or divorce him and thus held the authority had not considered this aspect. The court was alive to the fact that acceptance of the resignation may not necessarily put an end to the matrimonial wars, however, it recorded that accepting the resignation would be an effort to implement and afford protection to the right to family of the petitioner.

Though there can be no legal flaw that can be pointed here, but an interesting question that does come to mind is whether it is the employers' lookout to take care of the family issues of their employees? Since one might argue that a great investment goes into employees on part of the employers and should there be no responsibility on the part of the employees to keep apart the personal from the professional?

Another interesting angle explored by the court was that all the statutes that regulate marriage in India make it mandatory for the court to make an effort to bring about reconciliation between the parties. The court held it to be a mandate for every court and authority to attempt reconciliation between warring spouses. The high court cited the Supreme Court[6] where it was held that:

The sanctity of marriage is, in essence, the foundation of civilization, and therefore, court and counsel, owe a duty to society to strain to the utmost to repair the snapped relation between the parties.

It concluded by holding that,

> . . . *it shall be the duty of the court in the first instance in every case where it is possible to do so consistently with the nature and circumstances of the case, to make every endeavour to bring about a reconciliation between the parties.*

The court went on to hold that the effort of reconciliation has been statutorily institutionalized, and given the importance of marriage, the acrimony between spouses' manifested erosion of the basic human rights of the persons involved and impacted the community as well as society.

However, in the same paragraph, the court also mentioned that an effort for reconciliation may result in the parties burying their differences or parting. In either case, stability would be brought to their lives and the parties would know where their relationship stood, and the litigation would be culminated. This observation is indeed welcome. With this, the court recognized that though *family* serves as an important constituent, it is not necessary to continue living in a failing relationship. After all, the family as a basic unit can serve its purpose most effectively when it itself is not based on acrimony.

The court very logically concluded that the instructions are perfectly in tune with the international covenants and jurisprudence. And hence, the desire of the petitioner to try to resolve disputes and cohabit with her husband and daughter, as a family, needs to be protected. It was observed that her employment was not only interfering with the same but had become the root cause of such discord leading to a threat of severance of her matrimonial ties on account of dissolution of her marriage by a decree of divorce.

Laudable though it might be, the attempt by the court to save the very fundamental block of society, one cannot but stop to pause and think whether the court, while examining the situation, took into account the husband and his job choices. Is it the wife alone on whose shoulder the onerous duty of protecting the family and matrimony lies? Did the court make an attempt to resolve the dispute through the means of official mediation? This again brings Kalpana Chawla, referenced in the opening part of this essay, to one's thoughts, whose husband's support never wavered. They both shifted to Boulder, USA, where she had enrolled for her doctoral programme, and her space missions often took her away from family.

Yes, 'The times They-Are-A-Changin'', but in the Indian scenario, by and large, fortunate are the women who are 'allowed to work' after marriage. Unfortunately, many women themselves believe in being grateful to their husbands' families, and such are the 'values' engrained since childhood. 'Oh, you are working?', 'Isn't your family well off?' are some of the inane questions posed to working women even today. We may have come a long way, yet the sentiment that it is the woman's responsibility to take care of the household, children, husband and family has not yielded to the march of time. In many families, the working woman who dons multiple hats continues to be at the receiving end, genuinely holds guilt for not being able to meet unwarranted and sometimes impossible expectations, and yet we shall continue to come across many like Captain Krishna who truly believed it to be her fault for the tension in matrimonial life and was readily willing to give up her dreams and aspirations to save her marriage.

Thinking aloud, does this also not necessitate a fair and practical division of labour between the spouses, something which they need to openly discuss before taking the final step of tying the knot?

In conclusion, the court held the rejection of her resignation to be a gross violation of Captain Krishna's privacy and dignity, and hence her constitutional Right to Life guaranteed under Article 21, and also contrary to the spirit of the international covenants, other constitutional provisions, marriage laws of the country as also the specific army instructions. The court went on to render additional directions to the effect that a conciliation mechanism be explored and created by the government to facilitate resolution of disputes and differences, if any, in the areas related to marriage. It was observed that perhaps if such a facility was available, the officer may not have been in litigation. A direction was also given to the defence services to explore the institutionalization and putting into place a formal mediation and conciliation framework, perhaps within the existing welfare schemes or any forum for voicing grievances before the parties wrestle in courts.

And though one can find no fault in trying to save the marriage since it is undoubtedly an institution that serves an important purpose, the need of the hour also is to change the narrative. Along with educating young women, it would serve us well to teach our young men as well that marriage should no longer be understood in terms of the stereotypical gender roles.

I would add that for society as a whole, it might be time for introspection. It is time that duties and obligations in marriage are not dictated by socially and culturally ordained gender norms; where each spouse has the freedom to work or not, a choice driven by personal and individual preferences rather than societal expectations; where the father can also take time out during the child's exams; where each respects the others' job, irrespective of the earnings; where it is not just the wife who has to sacrifice her work in order to move with her husband on transfers and shifts; where she is supported by her spouse at home in order to be fully armed to break the glass ceilings at work; where spouses take turns to cook and clean; where girls, driven by the patriarchal set-up are not constantly looking for boys who are doing better than them; where girls do not feel the necessity to marry in the first place; where unmarried and/or single women are not viewed differently in our society; where women who try to break free of the societal shackles of gender are encouraged instead of being punished; where a woman is defined not by her gender but her own intrinsic self; where a woman has no need to break down walls and gender stereotypes; where constitutional guarantees of equality become a reality, without resorting to litigation!

I may be criticized for there is not a word of succour about the poor husbands who assume women to be their personal property and take on the entrenched roles of being the breadwinners while the wife takes care of the household. I think I am willing to take that risk. Let me illustrate. In case my husband were hypothetically to give up his profession and become a full-time stay-at-home dad, it would create quite a flurry and become a topic of 'discussion' in social groups, but on the other hand, if I took such a decision, it would not be perceived odd, and rather, in certain circles may evoke the sentiment that 'she has finally come to her senses!'. That explains it all.

To conclude, I would say that the conundrum is not really inherently about gender but socially assigned gender roles. Justice Sanjay Kishan Kaul, in minority of a five-judge Constitution Bench of the Supreme Court and speaking for himself,[7] quoted Bon Jovi's 'It's my Life' to emphasize the choice of non-heterosexual couples to love. It equally applies here. After all, it is about us feeling empowered enough to follow our own dreams and aspirations; to have the requisite strength, courage and belief in our own selves; and to make a choice and act as per our own freedom. And this is exactly what the Delhi High Court did, it stood behind Captain Krishna and her decision to give it all up and live with her family. After all, it is *her* life.

10

Rethinking 'the Woman Question' in the Indian Legal System

K. Parameshwar and Arti Gupta

Kush Kalra v. Union of India

Problems of 'social injustice' in the world are increasingly viewed as problems to be *acted upon*. Newer disciplines like 'poor economics' and 'development engineering' are sought after choices at universities,[1] the idea of 'ethical capitalism' is the purported foundation of the pervasive microfinance industry[2] and no small part of techno-scientific research is now geared towards increasing the economic share of each life.[3] The aspirations to *take action*, *do good* and *make a difference* are now the first steps to actively fill in the insufficiencies of the world.

The domain of gender (in)justice is not isolated to this. It is no coincidence that 'the woman question'—which encompasses all articulation(s) of how gender affects life—is always posed as a question to be *resolved*.[4] When all debates on women are directed towards action—*improving* the status of women, *ameliorating* gender injustice, *countering* heteropatriarchy, *resolving* the woman question—then any history of gender remains relevant only to the extent it illuminates these outcomes. Thus, all gendered history is reduced to either a history of gradual 'progress' or 'decline'.[5]

This reductive linearity appended to gender, either progressing or declining, sutures *Kush Kalra*[6] as well. While the immediate concern before the Delhi High Court in *Kush Kalra* was the exclusion of women from the Territorial Army[7] in India, the judgment implicitly presented itself as a seamless culmination from a spate of judicial decisions that have progressively conferred a previously unavailable right or entitlement on women. In the subsection titled 'Judicial recognition of the greater role of women in all spheres of life', *Kush Kalra* surveyed the lineage that it suggestively portrayed itself to be furthering. Beginning with *Muthamma*,[8] it highlighted Justice Krishna Iyer's reprimand to the 'misogynous posture' that was a 'hangover of the masculine culture of manacling the weaker sex forgetting how our struggle for national freedom was also a battle against woman's thralldom'. Thereafter, it chronologically dwelt on *Anuj Garg*,[9] then *Babita Puniya*,[10] *Charu Khurana*,[11] and finally, *Annie Nagaraja*.[12] It, therefore, comes as no surprise that what *Kush Kalra* gathered from these precedents are not just tight legal principles, but sweeping gendered remarks. To illustrate, *Kush Kalra* took note of *Anuj Garg* on the following dictum:

30. In the pronouncement reported at (2008) 3 SCC 1, *Anuj Garg v. Hotel Association of India*, the Supreme Court was concerned with a challenge to the Constitutional validity of Section 30 of the Punjab Excise Act, 1914… Some observations of the Court which may have a bearing on the consideration in the present case deserve to be extracted *in extenso* and read thus:

34. The fundamental tension between autonomy and security is difficult to resolve. It is also a tricky jurisprudential issue. Right to self-determination is an important offshoot of gender justice discourse . . .

"Stereotype roles and right to options

41. Professor Williams in The Equality Crisis: Some Reflections on Culture, Courts and Feminism published in 7 WOMEN 'SRTS.L. REP., 175(1982) notes issues arising where *biological distinction between sexes is assessed in the backdrop of cultural norms and stereotypes.* She characterises them as "hard cases". In hard cases, the issue of biological differences between sexes gathers an overtone of societal conditions so much so that the real differences are pronounced by the oppressive cultural norms of the time. This combination of biological and social determinants may find expression in popular legislative mandate. Such legislations definitely deserve deeper judicial scrutiny. *It is for the court to review that the majoritarian impulses rooted in moralistic tradition do not impinge upon individual autonomy. This is the backdrop of deeper judicial scrutiny of such legislations world over.*

42. Therefore, one *issue of immediate relevance* in such cases is the *effect of the traditional cultural norms* as also the *state of general ambience in the society which women have to face while opting for an employment* which is otherwise completely innocuous for the male counterpart. In such circumstances the question revolves around the approach of the State."[13]

One notices the slippage to the extra-legal threshold of political theory—the theorization of stereotypes, norms and societal ambience. *Kush Kalra* tied the litany of precedents it surveyed not on the basis of what they said about discrimination within defence services, or the State's abdication of its responsibility towards gender equality, but on the basis of what they encapsulated about women bettering their position in life. *Kush Kalra* concluded this survey with Lord Denning's words:

A woman feels as keenly, thinks as clearly, as a man. She in her sphere does work as useful as man does in his. She has as much right to her freedom to develop her personality to the full as a man. When she marries, she does not become the husband's servant but his equal partner. If his work is more important in life of the community, her's is more important of the family. Neither can do without the other. Neither is above the other or under the other. They are equals.[14]

A legal judgment isn't just a standalone decision; it also connects to earlier cases. *Kush Kalra*'s intervention isn't just about following old rulings but about actively using the law to support gender equality. Even *Kush Kalra*'s choice to begin with an excerpt from John Stuart Mill's *The Subjection of Women*, widely considered to be the one of the foremost feminist texts of the Western world, was no stray choice.[15] It was the first indication of the judgment's spillover from the domain of 'pure' law to the domain of progressive politics. One cannot help but remember Duncan Kennedy's pithy remark that legal reasoning is nothing but the path between 'the law' and 'how-I-want-to-come-out'.[16]

It might be misplaced to rebuke something for measuring itself at the touchstone of (gender) progress. 'Modernity' and 'development', as world-making projects, are nothing but measures of progress/regress themselves,[17] and this world never tires of them. It might also be misplaced to be critical of a judgment for spilling over into politics. If judgments have any *expressive* function,[18] or any *social* meaning, then expectation of some pristine legality is absurd to begin with. Hence, what is so unsettling about viewing women's history, and their lives, as a measure of societal progress or decline, as *Kush Kalra* tends to do?

In the context of British colonialism in India, an answer would be that the tussle over women-centric progress has historically been a tussle over the right to subjugate. Historical accounts of British India, especially those spanning the mid-eighteenth to the mid-nineteenth centuries, increasingly make it explicit that the moral legitimacy of colonialism was premised on the socially backward position of women in the Indian subcontinent, especially within Hindu culture.[19] When Katherine Mayo's *Mother India* made a case for the unfitness of Indians for self-governance, her raw material was India's 'social ills', especially their effect on women's position.[20] That Katherine Mayo 'shared the world's spotlight on India only with M.K. Gandhi'[21] is a testament to the remarkably wide appeal of her claim.

This charged significance of women's position was also exploited by anti-colonial forces. Upper-caste and upper-class Hindu nationalism invoked the authority, and selective reading, of scriptures to argue for Hinduism's past progressiveness on how it treated its women.[22] Thus, the ideological apparatus for colonialism and the anti-colonial arguments for self-governance were both premised on the political import of women's position in the colony. This is not to say that women were not oppressed, or that such oppression was only a figment of colonial imagination, but that the actuality of women's oppression was bracketed in favour of either vindicating European control or Nationalist thought.[23]

If gender provided a part of the ideological apparatus for imperialism, then law, or rather the absence of it, provided another. To borrow from Bernard Cohn:

> *Although it was recognized that there was 'law' in India, that 'law' was believed to be different from the European kind.* Because the government was seen as based on 'no other principle than the will of one *[the Mughal]*,' the *law was based upon his will* . . .
>
> In summary, the model of the Mughal-Indian political system was absolute and arbitrary power, unchecked by any institution, social or political and resting in the persona of the emperor, with property and honors derived solely from the will of the despotic ruler. *The idea that India had been ruled by 'despots' was revalorized in the nineteenth and twentieth centuries as one of several ruling paradigms that formed the ideological infrastructure of British Rule in India.*[24]

Accordingly, the woman and the law became two nails in the coffin that buried Indian self-governance. Thus, colonial subjugation not only had at its epicentre the position of *women*, but also found its baton in women-centric *legislations*—the Sati Abolition Act, 1829, the Hindu Widows' Remarriage Act, 1856, and the Age of Consent Act, 1891, amongst others.[25] When viewed against this backdrop, a stark intimacy between law, politics and the state, is seen to be playing out on the canvas of gender.

The law, especially law on women, as an overt attempt to *better* their position—an attempt at progress—became the primary signifier of imperial governance.[26] That women were never intended to be the beneficiary of such legislations became an ancillary detail.

If one were to accelerate the above timeline, one would notice that despite this fraught political beginning of women-centric legislations, so tainted with the hegemony of colonialism,[27] laws on women ultimately became the vector of how women themselves bargained with the colonial and postcolonial state. With the advent of the twentieth century, for instance, a shift is perceptible. Ambitious women's organizations such as the Women's Indian Association (WIA, 1917), the National Council of Women in India (NCWI, 1925) and the All India Women's Conference (AIWC, 1927) began to constitute women into a collective, albeit an upper caste/class one.[28] These collectivities, amongst which AIWC was to prove to be the most enduring, also mobilized around legislative reforms in the domain of child rights, divorce and inheritance, female labour, trafficking, etc.[29]

Over time, with the possibility of an independent nationhood on the horizon, anti-colonial organizations, including the AIWC, were also articulating women's subjectivity to be that of *citizens* of the budding nation.[30] There was a general fervour, propelled by anti-colonial sentiments, to contribute to the nation and its progress. The draft of *Indian Woman's Charter of Rights and Duties* prepared by Hansa Mehta, Rajkumari Amritkaur and

Lakshmi Menon, and submitted to the United Nations
Economic and Social Council in 1946, powerfully called
upon the women's collective:

1. To come forward in large numbers to take to these
   essential services;
2. To come forward for work in time of national need;
3. To educate themselves for good citizenship;
4. To fight against the social evils which retard the
   progress of this country such as child marriage, purdah,
   polygamy, caste communalism, untouchability, etc.;
5. To educate and bring up children if any to become
   good citizens;
6. To set and maintain a high standard of morality in all
   spheres of life; and
7. To strive to the utmost for world peace.[31]

The desire was that Indian women's status must be
'improved and brought on a par with that of man so that
she may contribute her legitimate share to the general
reconstruction of the life of this country and to a wider
world'. Such demands, it was specifically stated, must 'form
the basis of future legislations'.[32] While previously enabling
the colonial state's legitimacy, social reform legislations for
women ultimately came to represent the self-governing
capacity of the emerging nation. While the earlier spell of
legislations on sati and widow remarriage were intended
to solidify the legitimacy of the colonial state, the demand
for new legislative reforms by women's collectives sought

to invert that legitimacy and represent the 'potential of a modernizing national state in India'.[33]

Some questions must be grappled with here. Is this shift from the hegemonic underpinnings of the earlier women-centric legislations to women themselves reclaiming the legal language just another instance of the linearity of women's progress? If law was, since its inception, a tool of colonial rule, why would the 'native' population, especially women, repose any faith in it to begin with? How are pervasive realities of women's oppression to be reconciled with their entrance in public spaces and public organizations to talk the language of rights and legalities? Elizabeth Kolsky provides the starting point to think about these questions. Despite assertions of equal justice and rule of law, the administration of colonial law to the native population was certainly biased against the native. Nevertheless, the aspirational promise of colonial justice offered a language and a rhetoric to critique the rulers themselves:

> On the one hand, the special rights and privileges provided by law to European British subjects normalized and enabled their brutality. On the other hand, the terror induced by individual Britons uncovered the violent basis of imperial power and created a terrain for claims-making and critique. *Even though the gap between the promise of equal justice and the practice of something different produced startlingly biased legal decisions, it also exposed the government to the criticism of a variety of*

historical actors in India and abroad. The publicity devoted
to white violence and the efforts to control it suggest that
while the legal system may not have been equal or impartial,
the promise of colonial justice did restrict the gross exercise
of power by offering a language and a means to imprison
India's rulers within their own rhetoric. In this way,
colonial justice sustained and destabilized the empire at
once.[34]

However, a word of caution here. This shift must not be
reduced into a dialectical relationship between the earlier
domination of law, and women's later reliance on law's
counterinsurgent possibilities.[35] Neither is history so neat,
nor oppression (gender or colonial) so quickly fixed. To
believe so would be to fall for the lure of wanting to *resolve*
the woman question.[36] The frictions between women's
domesticity and their emerging professional aspiration,
between the idealization of the mythical Sita and Savitri
and the pulls of a modernizing influence, between the
increased control of women's sexuality and their visible
emergence in public spaces,[37] and most importantly, the
simultaneity of all of this remained an 'unresolved state of
affairs, or a state of ideological disharmonies, rather than
one of a resolutionary synthesis'.[38]

Hence, *how* women 'worked' the law cannot be pinned
to a straight line of events. The only surety is that they
did, a surety that structured postcolonial India's combat
with gender injustice. The starting point of this, on the
eve of formal decolonization in 1947, was the radical

report published by the subcommittee on Women's Role in Planned Economy. Published under the aegis of the National Planning Committee, the report recognized several intertwined areas for *State-led* economic equality of women.[39] In its ambition of nation-building, the report averred that the State must consider the planned economy with women as the focus. And the *legislative* means of the new nation was instrumental for this project. The Towards Equality Report, 1974, as independent India's most impactful account of women's position, also envisaged the legislative domain to be a significant propeller of women's equality.[40] Illustratively, Prabha Kotiswaran has argued that:

> Feminist engagement with regulatory reform in the 1980s generated several successes when laws against rape, dowry deaths, sati, sex selection of fetuses, and sexist media representations were passed . . .[41]

Consequently, the postcolonial Indian women's movement entrenched its faith in the law. Its demand was not for the state to recede, as the conventional understanding of human 'rights' now indicates,[42] but for the state to step up and legislatively intervene.[43] Thus, the law, as an erstwhile tool of imperial subjugation, became the primary tool of postcolonial feminist negotiation. Legal progress, therefore, came to be a placeholder for feminist progress.

The image of the State as a benefactor and enabler undoubtedly ruptured when subaltern voices (or silences?)

brought to the fore the State's and its agencies' complicity in violence against women.[44] Mathura's gang rape within police custody,[45] the police's refusal to take Bhanwari Devi's suffering seriously,[46] or the torture, rape and murder of Thangjam Manorama while she was in the custody of Assam Rifles battalion[47]—these incidents affirmed that atrocities against women were also state-inflicted atrocities.[48]

Although these incidents showed the inadequacy of laws in emancipating women, enactment of new women-centric legislations was not halted, but spurred. Kalpana Kannabiran and Ritu Menon, writing in the shadow of state-led violence, elucidate that despite these instances, the women's movement augmented its engagement with the State, going beyond a demand for legislative change and becoming a direct participant in bringing it about:

The 1990s marked something of an unusual departure for the Indian women's movement as far as campaigning on issues was concerned. For one, terms and strategies like 'advocacy' and 'lobbying' began to be used much more commonly than before; parliamentarians and pressure groups were sought out to hear representations and field questions in Parliament; *women's groups engaged in discussions and organized campaigns with national and state commissions on women on several issues, ranging from sex work to child abuse and the impact of globalization on women*; and any number of 'gender sensitization' trainings were carried out with the judiciary, the police, bureaucrats. . . . In one sense, this 'mainstreaming' of women's issues marked an important break from the protest activism of the late 1970s and 1980s, when street demonstrations, demands for legal reform, and more direct confrontations with the state were much more in evidence.[49] (emphasis supplied)

This enduring engagement was neither delusional about the value of law, nor ignorant of state-led atrocity. It emerged out of an acuteness towards the possibility that 'purposive interaction with institutional machinery and systems' could still be critical for positive outcomes for women.[50]

Thus, several women-centric legislations from 1990s to 2010s owe themselves to Indian feminists' continued commitment and collaboration with the State's legal machinery.[51] Even with its glaring shortcomings, the legislative domain remained 'the most used and criticized sphere for thinking about justice for women'[52] in India. Interpreting this historical link between the law, State, gender and politics, one can conclude that gendered changes within the legal domain have been *legislative* changes, even if the emancipatory potential and political motive for those legislations could still be open to debate.[53]

Now, if the historical trajectory traversed above indicates that feminist ideas 'found more than a foothold in institutions of state power',[54] materializing in legislative changes, then how have the tides changed again in the present? The very act of choosing a subject of analysis implies that the subject is worth attending to. Therefore, the factum of an anthology on courts coming to 'her' defence being written now, and not before, bespeaks its own peculiarity. Books are not written on something already trite. That eight of the ten judgments in this anthology were written within the last decade is another testament to the novelty of this gendered emergence in courtrooms.

So, is the novelty of the present situation that a group erstwhile excluded from multiple arenas is being enfolded within? Or that a historically patriarchal entity (in our case, the Indian defence services) is now embracing women? These general phenomena now infuse every part of the world, which only makes our averment on triteness even more pertinent. Hence, what is so novel, original, exceptional about the woman being defended thus, as this judgment anthology frames?

If the implicit assumption underlying the present anthology is that *courts* are increasingly sensitive of gender, then what is visible is not simply courts' heightened consciousness, but also a visible state and legislative indifference to gender in the last ten years. As the cases in this anthology show, despite a judgment being rendered on an issue in one branch of defence service, legislative laxity still impelled petitioners from other branches to agitate the same issue before courts for their respective branches. To illustrate, all three judgments of the Supreme Court contained in this anthology pertain to the claim for Permanent Commission by women officers engaged in Short Service Commissions—*Babita Puniya*[55] (on Indian

Army*)*, *Annie Nagaraja*[56] (Indian Navy) and *Nitisha*[57] (Indian Army).

Even outside the bounds of this anthology, as recently as 2022, the Indian Army had sought to put severe restrictions on women's entry in Army Dental Corps.[58] Despite the decriminalization of adultery in *Joseph Shine*,[59] the Ministry of Defence had prayed for exemption from this decriminalization.[60] Even after the reading down of Section 377 of the Indian Penal Code in *Navtej Singh Johar*,[61] the Indian Army Act, and the Air Force Act still criminalize 'unnatural' conduct.[62]

Therefore, *not* law, but *legal adjudication* is the sole terrain on which feminist and queer causes are now precipitated in India. Even within legal adjudication, specific courts are the focal point for this precipitation—out of ten judgments that are the subject matter of this anthology, five have been rendered by the Delhi High Court, three by the Supreme Court, and one each by high courts of Punjab and Haryana and Madras.

Must this urge us to rethink not only *how* the Indian legal system resolves its 'woman question', but also what is the (narrow) *space* of this resolution? If debating women's position within the legislative sphere had its shortcomings, as sketched above, what value remains in resolving the woman question only within the confines of selective courtrooms? On the fiftieth anniversary of the Indian Supreme Court, Granville Austin beautifully articulated that 'in pursuit of the social revolution', the Supreme Court and the Parliament have persistently struggled against each other to retain custody of the Constitution.[63] However, today, during the seventy-fifth year of the Supreme Court, the state of affairs can only conclude that either the Parliament has ceded this custody, or that gender falls outside the ambit of social revolution it considers worthy of this struggle.

Some might also argue that this state of affairs is preferable because courts have been better custodians of the Constitution at least as far as 'sex' and 'gender' discrimination are concerned. The Indian Supreme Court has, in the last five years, conferred recognition on non-heteronormative acts and identities, rendered triple-*talaq* unconstitutional, granted women entry in a temple from which they had been historically excluded[64] and decriminalized adultery.[65] Courts have covered an unprecedented breadth from formal equality to non-discrimination, from substantive equality[66] to a frontal attack on gender stereotypes,[67] from explicitly acknowledging 'sexual autonomy'[68] to making agency a readily invokable legal principle.[69] All of this far exceeds any legislative promise of the past. In any case, some might add, the State's apparent concern for women in the past, manifesting in legislative changes, was only induced by popular outrage over violence against upper caste and/or upper-class women.[70]

Kush Kalra ultimately opened up the Territorial Army in India for women, and other judgments resolved myriad issues pertaining to women in the armed forces. However, considering the Indian State's fraught history with gender, particularly evident in State atrocities against marginalized women, does judiciary's exclusive dominion over gendered predicaments, and our unquestioning acceptance of it, further act to absolve the state of realizing constitutional promises? Does it serve to maintain gender as a 'non-issue' on the State's radar? Must past shortcomings be a cause to perpetuate utter indifference in the present? These are questions worth considering.

About the Contributors

Justice A.K. Patnaik is an Indian jurist and a former judge of the Supreme Court of India.

The son of Late Gopal Chandra Patnaik, a leading businessman of Odisha from the 1950s to the 1970s, Justice Patnaik did his schooling in Rajkumar College at Raipur and then read Political Science at the Delhi University. He relocated to Cuttack, Odisha and completed his LLB from the Madhusudhan Law College and joined the Bar at the Orissa High Court in 1974. He practised as an advocate in all branches of law, though his specialization was in commercial and constitutional law. He was the standing counsel of the State Road Transport Corporation and the senior standing counsel of the Odisha Commercial Taxes Organisation.

He was elevated as a judge of the Orissa High Court in January 1994 and was immediately transferred to Gauhati High Court in February 1994. After a tenure of eight years as a judge of Gauhati High Court, he returned to the Orissa High Court in April 2002. After a stint of about three years, he was appointed as the chief justice of the high court at Chhatisgarh and thereafter was transferred as chief justice of Madhya Pradesh High Court in October 2005. In November 2009, he was appointed as judge of the Supreme Court, where he remained until his retirement in June 2014.

Justice Patnaik was nominated by the Chief Justice of India to serve in prestigious roles, including as the chairperson of the Supreme Court Legal Services Committee and the chairperson of the Committee on Constitutional Law and Allied Subjects for the Indian Law Institute's project on restatement of Indian law.

He has been conferred with doctorate of law (Honoris Causa) by the Utkal University, Bhubaneswar, Ravenshaw University, Cuttack and National Law Institute University, Bhopal. He has been a visitor at the National Law University, Odisha at Cuttack and the National Law Institute University, Bhopal.

After his retirement from the Supreme Court, Justice Patnaik continues to deliver lectures and participates in various seminars and meetings concerning law and political science. He has revised the famous book by Justice G.P. Singh, *Principles of Statutory Interpretation*, the fourteenth edition of which was published in January 2016. He has also revised the widely referred D.D. Basu's *Shorter Constitution of India*, published in November 2017.

Justice Rajive Bhalla's journey through the court corridors commenced in 1978 when he joined the Bar of the Punjab and Haryana High Court.

He was elevated as a judge of the same high court in 2004, beginning a tenure that ended in 2016.

After retiring from the high court, he chaired two tribunals simultaneously. On completion of his stint at the tribunals, he returned to the Bar at the Supreme Court as a senior advocate.

Justice Bhalla is also dean, Department of Law at Guru Nanak Dev University, Amritsar, Punjab and his journey to explore the law continues. He considers himself lucky to be living in the times of great legal challenges and hopes that the good fight for the rights of humans continues.

Rajshekhar Rao is a senior advocate who practises law in Delhi. He is an alumnus of the National Law School of India University, Bangalore (1999) and has been an active litigator since then. He started his legal career with Indu Malhotra who later went on to become the first Indian woman to be directly elevated to the Supreme Court from the Bar. He then worked with senior advocate Gopal Subramaniam, whom he assisted as a junior counsel before the Tehelka Commission, as well as in the parliament attack case before the Delhi High Court and the Supreme Court of India. He has been in private practice since 2006 and was designated as a senior advocate by the Delhi High Court in 2021.

He lives in Gurgaon with his wife Sapna, their twins Agastya and Abhimanyu and their two adorable canines Cookie and Leo. When not wearing his customary black and white, Raj likes to play amateur photographer

(@photowaala_lawyer on Instagram) predominantly taking black and white pictures, shooting abstract photos and playing with light and shadows. He loves to travel and is a hardcore foodie apart from believing that he is an extremely good 'pun-*kaar*'.

His approach to life is 'if you stumble, make it part of the dance'. He takes pride in being the epitome of national integration having being born in Andhra Pradesh, growing up in Nagaland, studying at boarding schools in Shillong and Tamil Nadu and then completing the rest of his schooling from New Delhi, Bangalore and Secunderabad.

Francisca Pretorius is an international lawyer and senior consultant, and formerly the adviser and head of the Office of Civil and Criminal Justice Reform at the Commonwealth Secretariat, London.

She has also conceived, crafted and now leads the Commonwealth Secretariat's Military Justice Transformation project, assisting member countries in reforming their military justice systems.

With a diverse international career spanning corporate law in Johannesburg and the United States, lecturing in South Africa and Kenya and playing a key role at the Commonwealth Secretariat in the United Kingdom, she currently serves as a senior consultant at nRhythm, a US-based consulting firm. In this role, she advises entities internationally on regenerative law, governance and management. Licensed to practise law in South Africa and the US, Francisca merges legal expertise with a global perspective, advocating for justice and sustainability. She holds an LLB, an LLM in international trade law and an MBA in global, social and sustainable enterprise.

Professor (Dr) Shruti Bedi is director and professor of law, University Institute of Legal Studies, Panjab University, Chandigarh; international fellow, National Institute of Military Justice, Washington. D.C.; visiting professor, Faculty of Law, Universitas Airlangga, Indonesia; member, Executive Council, India International University of Legal Education and Research, Goa; and director, Centre for Constitution and Public Policy, University Institute of Legal Studies, Panjab University. She is the author of seven books, including *Terrorism: Our World & Our Laws* and *Indian Counter Terrorism Law*, and co-editor of five books, namely *Arrest and Detention in India: Law, Procedure & Practice*; *Judicial Review: Process, Powers and Problems*; *Taking Bail Seriously: State of Bail Jurisprudence in India*; *Law & Media*; and *The Electoral System*.

Her areas of research include specific issues under comparative public law, constitutional law, internal security law and organized crime. She has published seventy-eight articles in journals, books, blogs and newspapers. She is regularly invited for international and national lectures, media debates and panel discussions. She has lectured at Nottingham University and Nottingham Trent University, UK; University of Toronto, Canada; University of Ottawa, Canada; Pontifical Catholic University, Rio,

Brazil; Universitas Airlangga, Indonesia; Universitas Ubaya, Indonesia; and Ho Chi Minh City University of Law, Vietnam. She has been awarded with recognition as 'The Phenomenal She, 2022' by the Indian National Bar Association, New Delhi which acknowledges 100 women annually for their contribution to various fields in India. She has delivered a TEDx talk on 'Justice: The First Promise'.

Aishwarya Bhati is a senior advocate at the Supreme Court of India and currently the Additional Solicitor General of India. She is the youngest woman lawyer to be designated senior advocate by the Supreme Court. She also has the distinction of being one of the youngest Additional Solicitors General of India and the fourth woman to ever occupy this distinguished position.

She has passionately fought for women's rights, children's rights, rights of persons with disabilities. She has led from the front for the rights of women officers of the Indian Army, Indian Air Force and the Indian Navy for consideration of PC and command positions at par with male officers. She has been instrumental in leading the battle against the mighty tobacco industry on issues of larger pictorial warnings, plain packaging and stronger tobacco regulation.

Chitrangda Rastravara practises at the Supreme Court of India and is an advocate-on-record. She holds an LLM in human rights and has dealt with landmark cases relating to women in the defence services in the Supreme Court, besides representing the Union of India in many important matters.

She has also been a cadet with the National Cadet Corps (NCC) and has represented the State of Rajasthan as 'Best Cadet' at the Republic Day Camp in 2013.

Captain Loveleen Kaur Mann, with a career spanning two decades, is qualified in law and a proud Indian Army veteran. She has tackled intricate and critical issues across diverse areas, including court martial, litigation, regulatory compliance, policy advocacy and government affairs. She is currently working in a big tech company at a senior position.

Her legal journey began in the Judge Advocate General's department of the Indian Army, where she honed her skills in conducting court martial. This experience instilled in her a deep understanding of military law and the intricacies of legal proceedings. Following a successful stint in the army, she transitioned to the corporate world, managing complex litigation and regulatory compliance for a leading telecommunications company.

Her thirst for knowledge led her to further explore international law. She spearheaded legal research on international law projects, delving into complex legal frameworks and their practical implications. This experience broadened her perspective and equipped her with a global understanding of legal issues.

Beyond the courtroom and boardroom, Loveleen is a passionate advocate for policy development in emerging industries, especially the telecom-media-technology arena. Leveraging her legal expertise, she has championed policy advocacy in the creative, digital and sports economies, fostering positive change and growth for these dynamic sectors.

She holds degrees from prestigious institutions including Georgetown Law, Washington, D.C.; National Law Institute University, Bhopal; Officers' Training Academy, Chennai; Institute of Military Law, (now in) Delhi, and the Indian Institute of Management, Lucknow.

When not navigating the intricacies of the law, Loveleen finds solace in solving challenging crosswords, exploring museums and indulging in the thrill of skydiving.

Ratna Viswanathan is currently the chief executive officer at Reach to Teach, a social impact organization working towards improving teaching and learning outcomes in government schools. She is a former civil servant from the 1987 batch of the Indian Audit and Accounts Service.

Holding a master's in English literature, Ratna writes columns on diverse subjects such as development, governance and defence. Giving up a highly coveted career in the civil services to join the development sector, prior to Reach to Teach, Ratna has held leadership roles at various national and internation organizations. She also serves as an independent director on the boards of several companies. Ratna believes that the development sector gives one the flexibility and agility to bring long-term, systemic and transformational change to human lives.

In her current role, she is deeply passionate about making learning a joyful experience for students by fostering teacher-agency. She believes in learning out of curiosity and competing with oneself to achieve one's own potential. Working from within the existing education system, she seeks to create an environment that enthuses key stakeholders in a child's life. She believes learning happens when it is supported by an enabling environment.

She has closely followed issues related to gender in the government sector, especially in the defence services during her posting in the Ministry of Defence at New Delhi.

Anu Pal was enrolled as an advocate in the year 2007 and has served in the office of the Advocate General of Punjab in different positions from 2010–24 to represent the State.

Anu has dealt with matters involving challenges to State policy and laws, including interpretation of statutes, reservation laws, human rights, environmental issues, education, arbitration, rural development, licensing, taxation, stamp duty, mining, elections, service law and other innumerable matters.

She is also a trained mediator and a part of the mediation panel of the Punjab and Haryana High Court for conducting court-appointed mediations. She has been invited by different fora, including the University of Cambridge, the Judicial Academy, Chandigarh, and various colleges in India to speak on a range of topics.

Anu has travelled extensively, is a voracious reader loves music and loves getting lost in sylvan natural surroundings.

K. Parameshwar is a senior advocate at the Supreme Court
of India. He has been appointed as *amicus curiae* to assist
the Supreme Court of India in several landmark cases.
These include *Balram Singh v. Union of India* (manual
scavenging), *TN Godawarman Thirumulpad v. Union of
India* (Forest Bench for environmental matters), *All India
Judges Association v. Union of India* (pay and emoluments
of district judiciary), *Indian Young Lawyers Assn v. State
of Kerala* (entry of women into the inner sanctum of the
Sabarimala temple), *Mukesh v. State* (Nirbhaya gang rape
case), *In Re: Deficiencies in Criminal Trials*, and *In Re:
Expeditious Trial Of Cases Under Section 138 NI Act* (cheque
bounce cases) to name a few. He was conferred the Mukesh
Goswami Memorial Prize for exceptional performance in
the advocate-on-record examination in 2014. He holds a
BA, LLB (Hons) degree from the NALSAR University of
Law, where he was awarded nine gold medals for overall
excellence and outstanding performance in several subjects,
including constitutional law. He holds an LLM degree
from Jindal Global Law School and is currently pursuing
his PhD from National Law University, Delhi.

Arti Gupta is an advocate who has worked in the chambers
of K. Parameshwar and is currently pursuing further studies
at the Yale Law School. She graduated from National Law
School of India University, Bangalore, with a BA, LLB
(Hons) degree. She has written twice for the *Australian
Feminist Law Journal*, where one of her articles was chosen
as the winner of the Audre Rapoport Prize for Scholarship

on Gender and Human Rights awarded by the Rapoport Centre for Human Rights and Justice at the University of Texas. Apart from that, her essays have featured in *Supreme Court Cases Journal* (co-authored), *National Law School Business Law Review* (co-authored) and *Law and Other Things*.

Notes

Chapter 1: A Judicially Aided Leap Towards Equality

1   The *then* existing Women Special Entry Scheme was referred to as WSES.

2   *Babita Puniya v. Secretary* 2010 SCC OnLine Del 1116.

3   Select ranks are selection grade ranks of colonel and above which are attained by selection rather than by time scale.

4   Government of India, Ministry of Defence, Letter No 14(01)/2018-D(AG) dated 25 February 2019.

5   *Secretary, Ministry of Defence v. Babita Puniya* & Ors, Civil Appeals 9367-9369/2011 decided by the Supreme Court on 17 February 2020, reported at 2020 (7) SCC 469, para 28. Available at https://indiankanoon.org/doc/117198144/.

6   Ibid.

7   Criteria appointments are posts in the army which form a qualitative requirement and carry a higher value for subsequent promotions.

8   Command appointments involve proper command of military units or establishments as opposed to be posted in a 'staff' appointment under someone else in command.

9   Supra, note 5, para 87.

Chapter 2: A Footnote in the Battle for Equality?

1   *Union of India & Ors v. Lieutenant Commander Annie Nagaraja & Ors*, Civil Appeals 2182–2187/2020 decided by the Supreme Court on 17 March 2020, reported at 2020 (13) SCC 1. Available at https://indiankanoon.org/doc/25678827/.

2   Permanent Commission (PC) entitles officers to serve as a regular permanent employee till the age of retirement with full pensionary and service benefits.

3   *Roe v. Wade* 410 US 113 (1973) is a 1973 decision of the Supreme Court of the United States which held that restrictive regulation of abortion by the government is unconstitutional. Available at https://supreme.justia.com/cases/federal/us/410/113/.

4   Short Service Commission (SSC) requires officers to serve for fixed terms of engagement in the defence services ranging from five to fourteen years after which they are compulsorily released from service.

5   LOK SABHA. (1957). The Navy Bill, 1957 (Report of the Joint Committee). Presented on 11 November, 1957, p. 27. Available at https://eparlib.nic.in/bitstream/123456789/58433/1/jcb_02_1957_navy.pdf.

6   Supra, note 1, para 78.

7   *Secretary, Ministry of Defence v. Babita Puniya & Ors*, Civil Appeals 9367-9369/2011 decided by the Supreme Court on 17 February 2020, reported at 2020 (7) SCC 469. Available at https://indiankanoon.org/doc/117198144/.

8   Supra, note 1, para 73.

9   Supra, note 7.

10 Supra, note 1, para 77.

11 Ibid., para 109.

Chapter 3: Discrimination, We See You

1   Jawaharlal Nehru, 'A Tryst with Destiny', speech delivered to the Constituent Assembly of India (14 August 1947).

2   Frost, R L. (1969). *Stopping by Woods on a Snowy Evening*. New York: Rineheart and Winston Inc.

3   *Babita Puniya v. Ministry of Defence* 2010 SCC OnLine Del 1116.

4   *Secretary, Ministry of Defence v. Babita Puniya* (2020) 7 SCC 469.

5   Ibid., para 67.

6   Ibid., para 74.

7   *Lt Col Nitisha & Ors v. Union of India & Ors*, Writ Petition (Civil) 1109/2020 decided by the Supreme Court on 25 March 2021, reported at (2021) 15 SCC 125. Available at https://indiankanoon.org/doc/190567716/.

8   Ibid., para 46–49.

9   *Griggs v. Duke Power Co* 1971 SCC OnLine US SC 47 wherein while dealing with the issue of employment criteria set out for candidates who were applying for a job at the respondent's power plant, it was observed that 'meaningful equality does not merely mean the absence of intentional inequality'.

10   *Madhu v. Northern Railways* 2018 SCC OnLine Del 6660, para 20.

11   Supra, note 7, para 48.

12   Ibid., para 71.

13   *Fraser v. Canada (Attorney General)* 2020 Supreme Court of Canada 28. Available at https://scc-csc.lexum.com/scc-csc/scc-csc/en/item/18510/index.do.

14   Supra, note 7, para 77.

15   *Coleman v. Attridge* 2008 IRLR 722 (ECJ), para 30.

16   Supra, note 7, para 137.

17   Ibid., para 50.

18   *Ontario Human Rights Commission v. Simpsons Sears Ltd* 1985 SCC On Linc Can SC 75, para 12.

19 Misc Application 1913/2022 in Writ Petition (Civil) 1109/2020 *Nitisha v. Union of India*

20 Supra, note 4, para 74.

Chapter 4: Pregnancy Discrimination in the Workplace—the Chasm between Law and Practice

1   'Women in Majority-Male Workplaces Report Higher Rates of Gender Discrimination', Pew Research Center, 7 March 2018. Retrieved on 05 March 2024 from: https://www.pewresearch.org/short-reads/2018/03/07/women-in-majority-male-workplaces-report-higher-rates-of-gender-discrimination/.

2   Krapf, M., Ursprung, H.W., and Zimmermann, C. (2014). 'Parenthood and Productivity of Highly Skilled Labor: Evidence from the Groves of Academe'. *Federal Reserve Bank of St. Louis Working Paper Series,* Working Paper 2014-001A.

3   Toussaint, L., and Webb, J.R. (2005). 'Gender differences in the relationship between empathy and forgiveness'. *Journal of Social Psychology,* 145(6), 673–85. doi: 10.3200/SOCP.145.6.673-686. PMID: 16334893; PMCID: PMC1963313.

4   McKinsey & Company, (2020). 'Diversity wins: How inclusion matters'.

5   *Monu Kumari v. Staff Selection Commission & Ors,* W.P.(C) No. 925/2017 decided on 3 April 2019 reported at 2019 SCC OnLine Del 8372. Available at https://indiankanoon.org/doc/12691143/.

6   *Laxmi Devi v. State of Rajasthan*, S.B. Civil Writ Petition No. 6305/2015, decided on 9 August 2019.

7   'Section 9', Constitution of the Republic of South Africa, 1996.

8   'Section 6', Employment Equity Act, 1998.

9   'Section 187', Labour Relations Act, 1995.

10 Schedule to the Basic Conditions of Employment Act, 1997.

11 Algoa FM, Feb 2016, Pregnant female soldiers takes SANDF to Equality Court. https://www.algoafm.co.za/domestic/

pregnant-female-soldiers-takes-sandf-to-equality-court;
Greeff, P, 7 May 2013, 'SANDF recruits severely assaulted
at Oudtshoorn infantry school – SANDU'. PoliticsWeb.
https://www.politicsweb.co.za/politics/sandf-recruits-severely-
assaulted-at-oudtshoorn-in; Sapa.

Mail & Guardian, 29 January 2013, 'Pregnant SANDF
women humiliated at Oudtshoorn military base'. https://
mg.co.za/article/2013-01-29-pregnant-women-humiliated-
at-oudtshoorn-military-base/.

12 414 U.S. 632, 94 S. Ct. 791 (1974).

13 *Crawford v. Cushman*, 531 F.2d 1114 (2d Cir. 1976).

14 Regulations were drafted after President Truman signed
Executive Order 10240 in 1951, which allowed the Department
of Defence to involuntarily discharge women who were
pregnant while serving, gave birth during service, or already
had children when joining the military. 'Defense Advisory
Committee on Women in the Services'. (2022). *DACOWITS
2022*. Department of Defense. Retrieved on 18 March 2024
from: https://dacowits.defense.gov/Portals/48/Documents/
Reports/2022/DACOWITS_2022_WebVersion_FINAL_
rev022123.pdf.

15 Supra, note 13.

16 Pregnancy Discrimination Act of 1978. Pub. L. No. 95-555,
92 Stat. 2076.

17 Defense Advisory Committee on Women in the Services.
(2022). DACOWITS 2022. Retrieved from https://
dacowits.defense.gov/Portals/48/Documents/Reports/2022/
DACOWITS_2022_WebVersion_FINAL_rev022123.pdf on
20 March 2024.

Chapter 5: Can Women Be Ambitious and Pregnant?

1 This extract is from a TEDx speech by Chimamanda Ngozi
Adichie, a critically acclaimed Nigerian author. It is available on

YouTube at: https://www.youtube.com/watch?v=hg3umXU_qWc.

2   The song is featured in Beyoncé's eponymously titled album released in 2013.

3   *Neetu Bala v. Union of India*, CWP 6414/2014 decided by the Punjab and Haryana High Court on 1 February 2016, reported at 2016 SCC OnLine P&H 602. Available at https://indiankanoon.org/doc/83563697/.

4   Ibid.

5   *Air India v. Nergesh Meerza* (1981) 4 SCC 335.

6   Supra, note 3.

7   Ibid.

8   *Union of India v. Ex Lt Selina John,* Civil Appeal 1990/2019, decided by the Supreme Court on 14 February 2024.

Chapter 6: Pregnant or Unwilling?

1   Smith, Nicholas. (2016). *Phenomenology of Pregnancy: A Cure for Philosophy?*. Sodertorn University.

2   Rich, Adreinne. (1976). *Of Woman Born: Motherhood as Experience and Institution.* New York: W.W. Norton and Company.

3   MacLeod, Denise Broughton. (March 2015) *Pregnancy as a source of discrimination: A Comparative study of anti-discrimination legislation in the European Union and the United States of America.* University of York.

4   *Inspector (Mahila) Ravina v. Union of India & Ors,* Writ Petition (Civil) 4525/2014 decided by the Delhi High Court on 6 August 2015, reported as 2015 SCC OnLine Del 14619. Available at https://indiankanoon.org/doc/170287517/.

5   Ibid, para 9.

6   Byron, Reginald A, & Roscigno, Vincent J. 'Relational Power, Legitimation, and Pregnant Discrimination'. *Gender & Society* 28, issue 3 (2014): 435–62.

7   Supra, note 4, para 12.

8   Ibid.

9   *Lt Col Nitisha v. Union of India & Ors* (2021) 15 SCC 125.

10   *Anuj Garg v. Hotel Association of India* (2008) 3 SCC 1.

11   Fredman, Sandra (2008). *Human Rights Transformed: Positive Rights and Positive Duties.* Oxford: Oxford University Press.

12   Supra, note 9, para 70.

13   Ibid, para 77.

Chapter 7: Leading the Charge or Lagging Behind?

1   *Handbook on Sexual Harassment of Women at Workplace (Prevention, Prohibition and Redressal) Act 2013*, Ministry of Women and Child Development, Government of India, November 2015.

2   *The Sexual Harassment of Women at Workplace (Prevention, Prohibition and Redressal) Act, 2013.* Available at https://www.indiacode.nic.in/handle/123456789/2104.

3   Farley, Lin. (1978). *Sexual Shakedown: The Sexual Harassment of Women on the Job.* McGraw Hill.

4   MacKinnon, Catherine A. (1979). *Sexual Harassment of Working Women: A Case of Sex Discrimination.* Yale University Press; Quinn, Beth A. (2002). 'Sexual Harassment and Masculinity: The Power and Meaning of a Girl Watching'. *Gender and Society.*

5   *Vishaka & Ors v. State of Rajasthan & Ors* (1997) 6 SCC 241.

6   Ibid.

7   *Shanta Kumar v. Council of Scientific and Industrial Research (CSIR) & Ors* 2017 SCC OnLine Del 11327.

8   Ibid.

9   *Aureliano Fernandesv. State of Goa & Ors* AIR 2023 SC 2485.

10   Supra, note 5.

11   Supra, note 9.

12   McLaughlin, Heather, Uggen, Christopher, and Blackstone, Amy. (2012). 'Sexual Harassment, Workplace Authority, and the Paradox of Power'. *American Sociological Review*.

13   Connell, RW (1987). *"Gender and Power: Society, the Person, and Sexual Politics."*. Stanford University Press.

14   *State rep by The Inspector of Police v. Commandant, Air Force Administrative College,* Criminal Original Petition 23403/2021 decided by the Madras High Court on 20 July 2023, reported at 2023 SCC OnLine Mad 4769. Available at https://lawbeat.in/sites/default/files/2023-07/ICC%20establishment%20in%20Armed%20forced-%20Madras%20HC.pdf

15   Ibid., para 40.

16   Ibid., para 46.

17   *Shital Prasad Sharma v. State of Rajasthan & Ors* 2018 SCC OnLine Raj 1676.

18   *Sarita Verma v. New Delhi Municipal Corporation & Ors* 2016 SCC OnLine Del 2362.

19   *M. Rajendran v. Daisyrani & Ors* (2018) 3 MLJ 84.

20   *Gaurav Jain v. Hindustan Latex Family Planning Promotion Trust & Ors* 2015 SCC OnLine Del 11026.

21   Armstrong, Elizabeth. A., Hamilton, Laura. T., and Sweeney, Brian. (2006). 'Sexual Assault on Campus: A Multilevel, Integrative Approach to Party Rape'. *Social Problems*.

22   Freyd, Jennifer J. (11 January 2018). 'When Sexual Assault Victims Speak Out, Their Institutions Often Betray Them.' *The Conversation.* Available at https://theconversation.com/when-sexual-assault-victims-speak-out-their-institutions-often-betray-them-87050.

23   Fitzgerald, Louise F, Suzanne Swan, and Vicki J. Magley. (2018). *But Was It Really Sexual Harassment? Legal, Behavioral, and Psychological Definitions of the Workplace Victimization of Women*. Boston: Allyn & Bacon.

24   Kawakami, Kerry. (2005). 'Kicking the habit: Effects of non-stereotypic association training and correction processes on hiring decisions'. *Journal of Experimental Social Psychology*.

25   Hart, Chole, Alison Dahl Crossley, and Shelly J. Corell. (2018). 'Study: When Leaders Take Sexual Harassment Seriously So Do Employees'. Business Management, *Harvard Business Review*. Available at https://hbr.org/2018/12/study-when-leaders-take-sexual-harassment-seriously-so-do-employees. Accessed on: 27 March 2024.

26   Supra, note 14.

27   Berdhal, Jennifer L. (2007). 'The Sexual Harassment of Uppity Women'. *Journal of Applied Psychologists*.

28   Berdahl, L.J, Magley, VJ, and Waldo, C. R. (1996). 'The sexual harassment of men: Exploring the concept with theory and data'. *Psychology of Women Quarterly*.

29   Burgess, D, and Borgida, E. (1999). 'Who women are, who women should be: Descriptive and prescriptive gender stereotyping in sex discrimination'. *Psychology, Public Policy, and the Law*.

30   Maass, A, Cadinu, M, Guarnieri, G, and Grasselli, A. (2003). 'Sexual harassment under social identity threat: The computer harassment paradigm'. *Journal of Personality and Social Psychology*.

31   Folke, Olle, and Rickne, Johanna. (2022). 'Sexual Harassment and Gender Inequality in the Labour Market'. Oxford University Press, *Quarterly Journal of Economics*.

32   Gruber, James. (1998). 'The Impact of Male Work Environments and Organizational Policies on Women's Experiences of Sexual Harassment'. *Gender and Society*.

Chapter 8: Challenging Bias and Gender Narratives

1   Bell Hooks. (2000). *Where We Stand: Class Matters*. Routledge. P. 45.

2   *Balvinder Kaur v. Union of India* Civil Writ 2708/90, decided by the Delhi High Court on 20 July 1995, reported at ILR 1997 DELHI 134. Available at https://indiankanoon.org/doc/1832702/.

3   Ibid.
4   *Lt (MNS) MM Sujaya, INHS v. Director General Military Nursing Service & Ors* 1991 SCC OnLine Ker 54.
5   *Indira Kumari Kartiayani v. The Maha Nideshak,* 1991 (2) SCC (SUPP) 149.
6   Supra, note 2.
7   Ibid.
8   *C.B. Muthamma v. Union Of India & Ors* 1979 AIR 1868.
9   Ibid.
10 *Vishaka & Ors v. State Of Rajasthan & Ors* (1997) 6 SCC 241.
11 *Mrs. Mary Roy et al. v. State Of Kerala & Ors* (1986) 2 SCC 209.
12 *Lata Singh v. State Of U.P. & Another* (2006) 5 SCC 475.
13 de Beauvoir, S. (1949). *The Second Sex.* Paris: Gallimard.
14 Jamison, S., and Witzel, M. (1992). *The Position of Women in the Vedic Ritual.* Cambridge: Harvard University Press.
15 Altekar, A.S. (1956). *The Position of Women in Hindu Civilization.* Banaras: Motilal Banarsidass.
16 Veil or curtain which is used to seclude women from public gaze.
17 Sharma, R.S. (1977). *The Social History of Ancient India.* New Delhi: Macmillan India.
18 *Manusmriti,* Verse 5.147. (200 AD). Delhi: Motilal Banarsidass.
19 Supra, note 13.
20 *Secretary, Ministry of Defence v. Babita Puniya* (2020) 7 SCC 469.
21 Press Information Bureau, Government of India, Ministry of Defence. (December 2022). Participation of women in defence sector. https://pib.gov.in/Pressreleaseshare.aspx?PRID=1882084.
22 Bakshi, D. (2006). 'In the Line of Fire: Women in the Indian Armed Forces'. New Delhi, India: *Women in Security, Conflict Management and Peace, Foundation for Universal Responsibility of His Holiness the Dalai Lama.*

23 *Union Of India v. Ex Lt Selina John*, Civil Appeal 1990 of 2019 decided by the Supreme Court on 14 February 2024.
24 Ginsburg, R.B. (5 May 2009). Interview. *USA Today*. Available at https://usatoday30.usatoday.com/news/washington/judicial/2009-05-05-ruthginsburg_N.htm.

Chapter 9: The Conundrum of Choice

1 *Captain (Mrs) Krishna v. Union of India & Ors*, Writ Petition (Civil) 166/2010 decided by the Delhi High Court on 8 October 2010. Available at https://indiankanoon.org/doc/167208227/.
2 Article 21 of the Constitution lays down, 'Protection of life and personal liberty: No person shall be deprived of his life or personal liberty except according to procedure established by law.' It would be pertinent to point out over here that Article 21 is one of the fundamental rights guaranteed by the Constitution of India and the Indian courts have at multiple occasions read various rights as an integral part of Article 21, e.g., right to privacy, safe environment, etc.
3 *Prem Shankar Shukla v. Delhi Administration* (1980) 3 SCC 526.
4 *Naz Foundation v. Government of NCT of Delhi & Ors* 160 DLT (2009).
5 *Major Rahul Shukla v. Union of India & Ors* 1995 SCC OnLine Del 548.
6 *V.K. Gupta v. Nirmala Gupta* (1979) 4 SCC 258.
7 Supriyo @ *Supriya Chakraborty & Anr v. Union of India* 2023 SCC OnLine SC 1348.

Chapter 10: Rethinking 'the Woman Question' in the Indian Legal System

1 Roy, Ananya, Gonzales, Genevieve, Agyemang, Kweku, and Talwalker, Clare. (2016). *Encountering Poverty: Thinking and*

Acting in an Unequal World. Berkeley: University of California Press.

2 Kar, Sohini. (2018). *Financializing Poverty: Labor and Risk in Indian Microfinance*. Stanford: Stanford University Press.

3 Murphy, Michelle. (2017). *The Economization of Life*. Durham: Duke University Press.

4 Mazumdar, Vina. (2010). *Emergence of the Women's Question in India and the Role of Women's Studies*. Retrieved on 19 February 2024 from https://www.cwds.ac.in/wp-content/uploads/2016/09/Emergence-Womens-Question.pdf.

5 Corfield, Penelope J. (2007). *Time and the Shape of History*. New Haven: Yale University Press.

6 *Kush Kalra v. Union of India*, Writ Petition (Civil) 10498/2015 decided by the Delhi High Court on 5 January 2018, reported at 2018 SCC OnLine Del 6439. Available at https://indiankanoon.org/doc/141300118/.

7 The Territorial Army (TA) is a part-time voluntary citizens' force where gainfully employed or self-employed citizens receive military training during their spare time for some days every year, so that they can bear arms for the nation in case of a war or national emergency.

8 *CB Muthamma v. Union of India* (1979) 4 SCC 260.

9 *Anuj Garg v. Hotel Assn. of India* (2008) 3 SCC 1.

10 *Babita Puniya v. Secretary, Ministry of Defence* (2010) SCC OnLine Del 1116.

11 *Charu Khurana v. Union of India* (2015) 1 SCC 192.

12 *Union of India v. Annie Nagaraja* (2020) 13 SCC 1.

13 Supra, note 6, para 31.

14 Supra, note 6, para 40.

15 Mill, John Stuart. (1869). *The Subjection of Women*. Peterborough: Broadview Press.

16 Kennedy, Duncan. (2008). *Legal Reasoning: Collected Essays*. Aurora: Davies Group Publishers.

17 Li, Tania Murray. (2007). *The Will to Improve: Governmentality, Development, and the Practice of Politics.* Durham: Duke University Press.

18 Sunstein, Cass R. (1999). 'Law's Expressive Function'. *The Good Society.* Available at https://www.jstor.org/stable/20710952?seq=1. Retrieved on 15 February 2024.

19 Sinha, Mrinalini. (2006). *Spectres of Mother India: The Global Restructuring of an Empire. Radical Perspectives.* Durham: Duke University Press.

20 Ibid.

21 Ibid.

22 Chakravarti, Uma. (1990). 'Whatever Happened to the Vedic Dasi (Recasting Woman)'. In Kumkum Sangari and Sudesh Vaid (eds), *Recasting Women: Essays in Indian Colonial History.* Rutgers University Press.

23 Bannerji, Himani. (2001). 'Pygmalion Nation: Towards a Critique of Subaltern Studies and the 'Resolution of the Women's Question''. In Bannerji, Himani, Shahrzad Mojab, and Judith Whitehead (eds), *Of Property and Propriety: The Role of Gender and Class in Imperialism and Nationalism.* Toronto: University of Toronto Press

24 Cohn, Bernard S. (1989). 'Law and the Colonial State in India'. In Starr, June, and Jane F. Collier (eds), *History and Power in the Study of Law.* Cornell University Press.

25 Nair, Janaki. (1996). *Women and the Law in Colonial India: A Social History.* New Delhi: Kali for Women.

26 Bannerji, Himani. (2002). *Inventing Subjects: Studies in Hegemony, Patriarchy, and Colonialism.* Anthem Press.

27 Guha, Ranajit. (1998). *Dominance without Hegemony: History and Power in Colonial India.* Harvard University Press.

28 Basu, Aparna, and Bharati Ray. (2018). *Women's Struggle: A History of the All India Women's Conference 1927-2016.* Manohar Publishers & Distributors.

29 Ibid.

30 Chetan, Achyut. (2023). *Founding Mothers of the Indian Republic: Gender Politics of the Framing of the Constitution.* Cambridge: Cambridge University Press.

31 Mehta, Hansa et al. (1946) *Draft of Indian Woman's Charter of Rights and Duties Prepared by India by AIWC.* 1 May. E/HR/ST/5.

32 Ibid.

33 Supra, note 19.

34 Kolsky, Elizabeth. (2010). *Colonial Justice in British India: White Violence and the Rule of Law.* Cambridge: Cambridge University Press.

35 Comaroff, John L. (2001). 'Introduction: Colonialism, Culture, and the Law: A Foreword'. *Law & Social Inquiry* 26(2): 305–14.

36 Chatterjee, Partha. (1993). *The Nation and its Fragments.* Princeton University Press.

37 Bannerji, Himani. (1995). 'Attired in Virtue: The Discourse on Shame (Lajja) and Clothing of the Bhadramahila in Colonial Bengal'. In Ray, Bharati (ed), *From the Seams of History: Essays on Indian Women.* Oxford: Oxford University Press.

38 Supra, note 26.

39 National Planning Committee. (1947). *Women's Role in Planned Economy.* Vora & Co, Publishers Ltd.

40 Guha, Phulrenu et al. (1974). *Towards Equality: Report of the Committee on the Status of Women in India.* Government of India. Available at https://pldindia.org/wp-content/uploads/2013/04/Towards-Equality-1974-Part-1.pdf. Retrieved on 19 February 2024.

41 Kotiswaran, Prabha. (2018). 'Governance Feminism in the Postcolony: Reforming India's Rape Laws'. In Halley, Janet et al. (eds), *Governance Feminism: An Introduction.* University of Minnesota Press.

42 Moyn, Samuel. (2010). *The Last Utopia: Human Rights in History.* Harvard University Press.

43 Matsuda, Mari J. (1989) *When the First Quail Calls: Multiple Consciousness as Jurisprudential Method.* 11 WRLR. Available at https://scholarspace.manoa.hawaii.edu/server/api/core/bitstreams/98224637-8c6b-4fa0-a31e-13fe5939db27/content. Retrieved on 15 February 2024.

44 Sharma, Sebastian. (2016) *'My face today is the face of Bastar's fight: Soni Sori'. The Hindu,* 9 March. Available at https://www.thehindu.com/news/national/otherstates/My-face-today-is-the-face-of-Bastar's-fight-Soni-Sori/article60504585.ece. Retrieved on 15 February 2024.

45 *Tukaram v. State of Maharashtra* (1979) 2 SCC 143; Letter from Upendra Baxi, Vasudha Dhagamwar, Raghunath Kelkar, and Lotika Sarkar to the Chief Justice of India (16 September 1979).

46 *Vishaka v. State of Rajasthan* (1997) 6 SCC 241.

47 Chakravarti, Paromita. (2010). 'Reading Women's Protest in Manipur: A Different Voice?' JPD 5. Available at https://www.jstor.org/stable/48603378. Retrieved on 15 February 2024.

48 Misri, Deepti. (2011). *'Are you a man?: Performing Naked Protest in India'. 36 Signs.* Available at https://www.jstor.org/stable/10.1086/657487?seq=1. Retrieved on 15 February 2024.

49 Supra, note 41.

50 Ibid.

51 See the *Pre-Conception and Pre-Natal Diagnostic Techniques Act,* 1994; the *Protection of Women from Domestic Violence Act,* 2005; the *Protection of Children from Sexual Offences Act,* 2012; the *Sexual Harassment of Women at Workplace (Prevention, Prohibition and Redressal) Act,* 2013; and the *Criminal Law (Amendment) Act,* 2013.

52 John, Mary E. (ed). (2008). *Women's Studies in India: A Reader.* Gurgaon: Penguin Books.

53 Roy, Srila (ed). (2012). *New South Asian Feminisms: Paradoxes and Possibilities.* Zed Books Ltd.

54 Supra, note 41.

55 *Secretary, Ministry of Defence v. Babita Puniya* (2020) 7 SCC 469.

56 Supra, note 12.

57 *Lieutenant Colonel Nitisha & Ors v. Union of India & Ors* (2021) 15 SCC 125.

58 *Gopika Nair v. Union of India* (2023) SCC OnLine SC 1522.

59 *Joseph Shine v. Union of India* (2019) 3 SCC 39.

60 *Joseph Shine v. Union of India* (2023) SCC OnLine SC 149.

61 *Navtej Singh Johar v. Union of India* (2018) 10 SCC 1.

62 *The Army Act 1950*, s 46(a); *the Air Force Act 1950*, s 46(a).

63 Austin, Granville. (2004) 'The Supreme Court and the Struggle for Custody of the Constitution'. In Kirpal, BN et al. (eds), *Supreme But Not Infallible*. Oxford Academic, Online Edition.

64 *Indian Young Lawyers Association & Ors v. State of Kerala & Ors* (2019) 11 SCC 1.

65 Supra, note 59.

66 Supra, note 57.

67 Supra, note 61.

68 Supra, note 59.

69 *X v. Principal Secretary, Health and Family Welfare Department, Govt of NCT of Delhi* (2023) 9 SCC 433.

70 Debolina Dutta and Oishik Sircar (2013). 'India's Winter of Discontent: Some Feminist Dilemmas in the Wake of a Rape'. *Feminist Studies* 39 (1): 293.

Scan QR code to access the
Penguin Random House India website